THE PARTY GAME

THE
PARTY
GAME

—

William Crotty
Northwestern University

W. H. Freeman and Company
New York

Cover illustration Copyright © 1985 by David FeBland

Library of Congress Cataloging in Publication Data

Crotty, William J.
    The party game.

    Bibliography: p.
    Includes index.
    1. Political parties—United States.   I. Title.
JK2261.C8425   1985   324.273   84-18655
ISBN 0-7167-1602-X
ISBN 0-7167-1603-8 (pbk.)

1 2 3 4 5 6 7 8 9 0 MP 3 2 1 0 8 9 8 7 6 5

To Billy and Julie

Contents

Preface
∎

Political parties are in a state of flux. Their role, and the type of demands made on them, are changing. Much of what has been thought in the last generation to explain the dynamics of party operations appears irrelevant to an understanding of political parties as they function today, and as they must function in the future if they are to survive. The parties' contemporary environment is far less scrutable than the one that nurtured the New Deal party system, which dominated party politics from the early thirties to the late sixties.

The parties must adapt to the social and political forces released by a society that is questioning itself and, however haltingly, redefining its political life. The manifestations of this transformation are easily identified. Voters are more distrustful of all aspects of politics. Support for political parties and for governing institutions has weakened. There has been a revolution in campaign technology and operations—from overreliance on the media, especially television, to the emergence of corporate, labor, single-issue, and ideological PACs (political action committees). Party coalitions have become less institutionalized and party loyalties have weakened, with the result that party affiliation no longer determines election outcomes as it once did, especially among young voters. The closed presidential nominating process of a decade or two ago has been replaced with a participant-ori-

ix

ented, grass-roots emphasis, which has brought about a redesign of the forms and power distributions influential in presidential selection. The public financing of presidential elections, the creation of a federal watch-dog agency (the Federal Election Commission), and the strengthened campaign regulations of the post-Watergate period have reshaped campaign funding.

These factors, among others, characterize the political transformations now in progress. All have had their impact on the operations of the political parties.

This book attempts to provide some perspective on the changes taking place and their implications for the functioning, and relevance, of the contemporary party system. It examines the nature of the political parties' relationship to the society they serve and to the electorate they presume to represent (whose support they depend on) within a social and political environment that continues to undergo a basic redefinition. The book concludes with several speculations on the party system's future growth and capabilities.

For an enterprise like this to succeed, many people must contribute generously of their time and their ideas. Three colleagues were particularly helpful in their suggestions: Joel Goldstein, Richard Niemi, and Harold J. Spaeth.

William Crotty
Northwestern University

THE PARTY GAME

CHAPTER 1

Public Attributes and Party Support

■

Voters today, increasingly cynical toward politics, no longer place the trust in government institutions they once did. One result of this trend has been a sharp decline in voter participation: approximately one-half the electorate no longer votes in any election.

The effect on political parties is twofold. The environment in which the parties must operate has become increasingly hostile, while the parties themselves, never held in high esteem by the public, have continued to lose support, a factor that creates problems for the operation of parties and for society as a whole.

This chapter reviews these changes in public attitude toward politics and government and the decline in support for political institutions.

■■■■ ATTITUDES TOWARD GOVERNMENT, POLITICS, AND POLITICAL PARTIES

In the mid-sixties the major voting surveys considered eliminating questions relating to trust and faith in government and cynicism toward politics. The reason? The questions were expensive and the answers were consistently the same. People had a high degree of trust in government and they believed that government acted in the best interests of the majority of people.

1

Then something changed. Beginning in the early to mid-sixties, people became less supportive of government. They began to question the motives of political leaders and the fairness and helpfulness of government policies. This trend, which at first was tentative, strengthened and over the years voters turned increasingly distrustful of government, what it says, what it does, and whom it represents.[1] The following data illustrate the developments.

Table 1.1 traces the decline in trust in government. The trend has been pronounced. In 1958, when asked if "you can trust the government in Washington to do what is right," 57 percent of the people thought so (most of the time). By the late seventies, the figure was down to 27 percent. The most positive and the most negative responses can be combined and then subtracted from each other to gain a summary measure of the patterns over time (Table 1.1). When this is done, the shift in view is even more apparent. From a margin of +50 or better (positive views) in the late fifties and early sixties, there was a general decline by the mid-seventies (−30 by late in the decade).

Other measures of governmental trust reveal the same pattern (Table 1.1). While 64 percent of voters in 1964 believed that government was run for the benefit of all, by the late seventies there was a complete reversal in perceptions: 67 percent believed it was run by a few interests concerned only with their own welfare. In the late fifties, only 43 percent of the people felt the government wasted a good deal of tax revenue, while 37 percent thought government officials did not know what they were doing, and 70 percent believed that few government officials were crooked. By the late seventies, many if not most people felt the government wasted a lot of money, that government officials did not know what they were doing, and that government leaders were often crooks. Overall, while over one-half of the population could be scored among the most trusting in the late fifties, by the mid-to late seventies one-half could be counted among the most cynical, a complete reversal in attitude toward government.

The same pattern is repeated in still other measures of attitudes toward government and political processes, such as political efficacy (control over and ability to influence political events) measured both "internally" (self-perceptions of political ability) and "externally" (beliefs in the responsibility of official institutions); perceptions of government responsiveness; citizen duty or commitment to the obligation to vote in elections; and sense of

2

TABLE 1.1 ■ The Public's Trust in Government

	1958	1960	1962	1964	1966	1968	1970	1972	1974	1976	1978	1980
a. You can trust the people in Washington most of the time												
Percentage agree	57	—	—	62	48	54	47	48	34	30	27	26
Range	50	—	—	55	34	25	9	8	−26	−30	−39	−38
b. The government is run for the benefit of all												
Percentage agree				64	53	51	41	38	25	24	23	23
Range				35	20	12	−9	−16	−42	−42	−42	−54
c. The government wastes a lot of tax money												
Percentage agree	43	—	—	47	—	59	69	66	74	74	77	98
Range	9	—	—	4	—	−21	−39	−33	−50	−51	−57	−96
d. The people running the government don't seem to know what they are doing												
Percentage agree	37	—	—	27	—	37	44	40	46	50	51	35
Range	20	—	—	42	—	21	7	15	4	−6	−10	−30
e. Quite a lot of the people running the government are crooked												
Percentage agree	24	—	—	29	—	25	32	36	45	42	40	48
Range	46	—	—	38	—	46	34	24	6	11	15	5

Source: Center for Political Studies, University of Michigan, National Surveys. The data through 1978 are adapted from Warren E. Miller, Arthur H. Miller, and Edward J. Schneider, *American National Election Studies Data Sourcebook, 1958–1978*, Cambridge, Mass.: Harvard University Press, 1980.

political community (evaluated by a series of questions measuring trust in other people and used as an indirect measure of the cohesiveness of the population's attitudes).

A few points stand out. The proportion of people who believe they have no say in what the government does or that public officials don't care what people think has increased by about 50 percent since the fifties; the proportion who feel that government pays a good deal of attention to people's opinions before deciding what to do declined by better than one-half (32 percent to 14 percent); the proportion who consider elections a vehicle for influencing government decision-making is down; and the proportion who believe that congressmen place great emphasis on the views of their constituents is also down significantly (42 percent to 17 percent).[2]

On the other hand, and this may be seen as an anomaly, the public's sense of civic obligation (i.e., their belief that they have a duty to participate in elections) and their perceptions of the trustworthiness of others (the indicators of political community) have remained constant. The change has come in the public's attitudes toward political institutions. The public appears to be losing faith in its political processes and their responsiveness.

Lower income groups—those with the least formal education, blacks, blue collar workers, persons living in union households, farmers, and, in terms of party identification, independents—usually score lower on measures of trust and rate government responsiveness and efficacy lower than do other groups. However, the decline in support is society-wide.

Given the social and political upheavals of the last several decades—Vietnam, the violence of the sixties and early seventies (civil rights' slayings, political assassinations, burning cities, use of federal troops to quell domestic disturbances, Kent State, and the like), and Watergate—in addition to an ailing economy and the failure of either political party or a succession of presidential candidates to measurably improve the situation, it is little wonder that the public has lost a good deal of confidence in political institutions. The attitudinal developments appear to be a direct and not unrealistic response to a generation of turmoil.

Richard Jensen, a historian concerned with the interrelationship between politics and social, intellectual, and moral values, argues that the transformation of views began with the young and "may well involve a systematic rejection of modern values on the part of the well-educated youth of America." Jensen explains:

The signs started appearing in the late 1950s and early 1960s growing rapidly after 1963. Youth demanded freedom from the tight psychological self-control demanded by the modern value system. The ideals of ambition, hard study, and upward mobility meant less and less to young people raised in an affluent society. Personal liberation meant marijuana, sexual experimentation, rock music, and radical activism. Patriotism lost its glamour in the mud flats of Vietnam. Ghetto riots, urban decay, support for reactionary dictatorships were all seen as indicators of the hypocrisy of modern values. Traditional life-styles, especially those of ghetto blacks, cast an irresistable charm.

. . . The cultural crisis began to spread rapidly to other age cohorts, abetted in part by the media. The economy seemed out of control: inflation, recession, food shortages, and energy emergencies came so fast that the public lost confidence in the experts of government, finance, and business. Disgrace, scandal, and humiliation tarnished the image of many local politicians, and of the Central Intelligence Agency, the Federal Bureau of Investigation, and even the White House, undercutting the modern faith in the capability of national leadership. Science and technology came under attack as interest in the occult blossomed. Rigid sex roles gave way, and even the institution of marriage was bypassed. In a word a loose set of "postmodern" values emerged, drawing support from the best-educated groups than once were the mainstay of modernity and Republicanism. . . .

Perhaps the most important impact of the postmodern challenge lies in the rapid spread of cynicism and apathy. Today fewer people identify closely with political parties than ever before in the 150-year sweep of history surveyed. . . . Fewer people vote, and fewer people care. The result may well be that government power increasingly is concentrated in the hands of civil service bureaucrats and judges who do not see themselves as duty bound to express the popular will in their decisions. If that

5

comes to pass, the world's first democratic polity will have abandoned its heritage.[3]

One does not have to agree with all of Jensen's points to appreciate the central thesis: there has been a decided transformation in American political values. The picture is not encouraging, and it directly affects the way in which the public views political parties.

■■■■ PUBLIC PERCEPTIONS OF POLITICAL PARTIES

The change in the public's attitudes has directly affected its acceptance of and support for political parties. Never strong, the public's good will toward the party system has been severely tested. Jack Dennis, perhaps the most prominent student of these developments, has written: "From the earliest beginnings of the American nation, the legitimacy of the institution of the political party has always been open to question."[4] By the mid-seventies Dennis was arguing that "the parties are clearly and sharply on the wane as an important feature of American politics. Indeed . . . the party institution has entered a period of rapid decline which could well be followed by its demise."[5]

The signs are truly ominous. The public's attitudes—based on their perception of political parties, specifically, the parties' attentiveness to people's opinions and the extent to which parties, in turn, can make government responsive to its citizenry—show an erosion of support. Once mildly favorable impressions have now turned negative.

When political parties were compared with other institutions in relation to public trust, in a series of questions occasioned by the Watergate crisis, the low levels of faith in these agencies became starkly apparent.

Ninety-eight to 99 percent of Americans would trust the presidency, Congress, or the Supreme Court before they would trust parties. Conversely, roughly 60 percent of the population trust parties the least. An average spread of almost 50 percentage points separates parties from the next *least*-trusted political institution.[6]

In a more intensive analysis of his continuing polling of the Wisconsin electorate's evaluations of its parties, Dennis found that
parties were believed to create conflict rather than diffuse it and

to confuse issues rather than clarify them. He found that there was even a declining support for presenting party labels on the ballot (in fact, by 1976 in a complete turnabout from the mid-sixties, the Wisconsin public opposed this). Eighty-nine percent of the Wisconsin sample agreed that a voter should make a choice on the basis of the candidate and his qualifications, not party label, and 79 percent disagreed with the statement that a senator or representative should follow his party's leadership if he does not want to.[7]

Wisconsin has always had a strong tradition of political independence and this may color the responses. More than likely however, they are broadly representative of the tone and direction of the political attitudes associated nationwide with the party system.

Dennis is one of the few political scientists who have attempted systematically to trace the support patterns for the party system (Figure 1.1). His model is divided into long-run acculturation forces (e.g., childhood socialization to the political system, party identification, sense of political efficacy, and social class status) and shorter-run or more immediate experiences that relate to the contemporary political environment and work to shape perceptions and support patterns. For example, a decline in public confidence in political institutions would more generally affect the evaluation of parties, as would perceptions of the fairness of the system and its responsiveness to the needs of a particular individual. In another context, the feelings of a committed partisan, actively engaged in party work, can be expected to be different from those of an individual untouched by the party system.

Dennis includes these measures in his model. As he shows, "diffuse support"—an indicator of long-term support for the assumptions of the governing system, a product of previous politicization experienced in the home, the school, and the community—has the most direct impact on party support patterns. These attitudes are, in turn, correlated with and reinforced by other long-run factors such as party identification, political efficacy, and socioeconomic status. Dennis writes:

> The people most likely to remain supportive of the
> party system during this period of
> deinstitutionalization are those higher in social status,
> have a stronger partisan self-image, have greater
> political efficacy, support the regime of democracy in

7

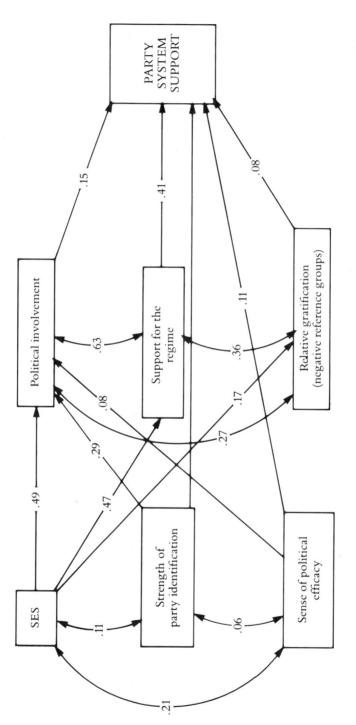

FIGURE 1.1 ■ Factors contributing support for the party system. (From Jack Dennis, "Changing Public Support for the American Party System," in *Paths to Political Reform*, William Crotty, ed., Lexington, Mass.: Lexington Books, D. C. Heath, 1980, with permission.)

general, are more politically involved, and feel less hostility toward other groups who share in the struggle for benefits available in American society. These are among the most important attributes of those who retain support while general support for political parties continues to decline.[8]

This is the one group broadly enthusiastic about political parties. It is a relative minority within the general population, which over-all has seen its confidence in the party system shaken. Public support for the parties continues to decline. The attachments of the pro-party elements of the population and, conceivably, the continuing efforts at party and broader political reforms (a more debatable proposition) may be "only postponing the evil day of total collapse" of the contemporary party system.[9] If this were to occur—and the possibility is there—it would be a sad day for American politics.

■■■■ CONCLUSION

E. E. Schattschneider has argued that "the political parties created democracy and that modern democracy is unthinkable save in terms of the parties."[10] Without question, political parties provide invaluable services for a democratic polity. For example, political parties—

- organize public coalitions of relatively like-minded citizens behind candidates and policies in general accord with their views and needs.

- select, through their nominating procedures, and then promote, through general election campaigns, the political elite who will run the public institutions of government.

- hold (at least theoretically) those in office accountable and responsive to the citizens who elected them.

- provide alternatives that allow the voter the ultimate choice concerning the direction and substance of public policy.

- link the government with the electorate, an intermediary function of inestimable consequence.

- educate the population about the limits of government, the duties of citizenship, and its role in a democratic polity.

- ■ limit the power of those in authority through informal checks and a responsible exercise of the options available to the opposition.

- ■ provide the basis for a more cohesive functioning of a governmental system formally based on a federalized and separation-of-powers approach to power.

- ■ create the coalitions, inside the legislature and out, necessary for the adoption of relatively coherent and representative policy initiatives responsive to the types of issues and concerns that lead to a party taking office.

There are other functions—in fact, the services that a vital party system provides for a political system are virtually endless—but these are its major contributions to democratic governance. They are substantial, and it is difficult to envision an equitable and representative polity without productive and healthy political parties.

Walter Dean Burnham, possibly the most prominent student of political party decline, would add another point:

> Political parties with all their well-known human and structural shortcomings, are the only devices thus far invented by the wit of Western man which with some effectiveness can generate countervailing collective power on behalf of the many individually powerless against the relatively few who are individually—or organizationally—powerful. Their disappearance could only entail the unchallenged ascendancy of the latter unless new structures of collective power were developed to replace them and unless conditions in the social structure and the political culture were such that they could be effectively used.[11]

It is a telling argument. The demise of political parties is not a prospect to be dismissed lightly. Still, it is up to the parties to *prove their relevance* within a changing social order. And a vital party system must do this over and over again. The parties must adapt to meet new demands. It is their job to reassert their primacy in the political arena—now seriously challenged—and to establish (if that is the right word) a confidence in their capacity to be representative, accountable, and responsive to the needs of a nation undergoing change. Meeting such challenges will not be easy.

CHAPTER 2

Political Participation and Voter Turnout

■

Political involvement is on the decline. The result is an electorate decreasing in size (the support of roughly 27 percent of the electorate in 1980 could have decided whether Carter or Reagan held office) and more stratified to represent the wishes of a more selective, higher socioeconomic clientele.

Does it matter? Much depends on one's definition of democracy, what one considers to be the vital signs of a healthy political system, and how one interprets the changes in these. Many political scientists have long held the comfortable assumption that a relatively small (in cross-national terms) turnout indicates a contented and supportive citizenry. Passivity equals acceptance in this calculation. It is questionable if this is true today, or if it ever was. If it does explain the contemporary decrease in participation during troubled economic and social times, then we have an unusually acquiescent and understanding body of voters. If the traditional explanations do not hold, what does account for the lower levels of involvement and what do these levels say about the coming political era?

■ PARTICIPATION IN NATIONAL ELECTIONS

Voter turnout in presidential elections peaked in 1960 at 63 percent. Since then it has declined steadily and now hovers around 11

50 percent of the eligible electorate (Table 2.1). Turnout for congressional races has run about 4 percentage points behind the turnout for presidential contests in years when both offices were on the ballot and has run well below the presidential totals (10 to 20 percentage points) in off-year elections. In the early sixties, off-year House races drew about 49 percent of the voting age population. Since then participation has declined to a little over one-third of the electorate. In 1982 it was 37.6 percent, a slight increase over the 1978 off-year election (Table 2.1).

Thomas E. Cavanagh has intensively analyzed the changing nature of the electorate during the years 1968–1976.[1] By his calculations (Figure 2.1), while the size of the electorate increased by 40 million, the number of "core voters" (those participating consistently in elections) went up only 4 million while the total number voting increased by less than 7 million. At the same time, between 11 and 12 million former voters dropped out of the electorate in each of the presidential election years and an increasing imbalance of newly eligible adults opted not to participate. The number of core nonvoters virtually doubled (20.5 million to 38.6 million) while the total number *not* participating increased by over 20 million (59.9 million by 1976).

The figures themselves are alarming. A 159 percent increase in nonvoting over an eight year period represents a significant shift in electoral habits. While the number of traditional voters basically stabilized, the numbers of habitual nonvoters increased by a ratio of 4.5:1 over core voters. In another study, Walter Dean Burnham calculated that one-fifth of the active voting base in 1960 was not participating in elections by 1976.[2] Should the trend continue— dramatic increases in the total number of nonvoters, a stabilized drop-out rate, and the balance of the newly eligible not voting— the future may well find the majority of citizens not participating in elections at any level (presidential races have the highest turnout). The number of people completely outside the pull of elections exceeds the populations of any of the states and most nations.

The decline in participation has affected all major demographic and political groups—the young and the old, the rich and the poor, college and non-college educated, businessmen and laborers, blacks and whites, liberals and conservatives, Republicans and Democrats. Still, when the turnout figures are examined for each of the categoric groups in the electorate, differences do appear. The participation of certain groups has declined more rapidly and more substantially than others, while some groups, already

TABLE 2.1 ■ Turnout in Presidential and Congressional Elections, 1920–1980

Year	Republicans (%)	Democrats (%)	Year	Republicans (%)	Democrats (%)
1920	43.4	40.7	1952	61.6	57.6
1922	–	32.0	1954	–	41.7
1924	43.9	40.5	1956	59.3	55.9
1926	–	29.8	1958	–	43.0
1928	51.8	47.7	1960	62.8	58.5
1930	–	33.7	1962	–	45.4
1932	52.4	49.7	1964	61.9	57.8
1934	–	41.4	1966	–	45.4
1936	56.0	53.5	1968	60.9	55.1
1938	–	44.0	1970	–	43.5
1940	58.9	55.4	1972	55.5	51.9
1942	–	32.5	1974	–	36.2
1944	56.0	52.7	1976	54.3	49.6
1946	–	37.1	1978	–	35.5
1948	51.1	48.1	1980	53.2	47.9
1950	–	41.1	1982	–	37.6

Source: U.S. Department of Commerce, Bureau of the Census, *Statistical Abstract of the United States*, Washington, D.C.: U.S. Government Printing Office, 1972 and 1981. The data for 1920–1930 are from the 1972 edition; the data for 1932–1980 are from the 1981 edition.

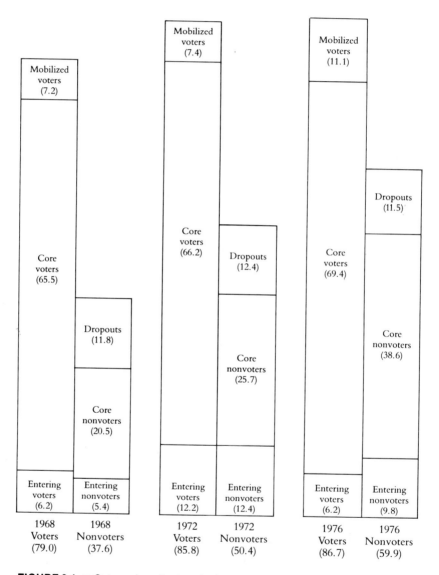

FIGURE 2.1 ■ Categories of voters in the electorate, 1968–1976. Numbers represent civilian noninstitutional population, in millions. (After Thomas E. Cavanaugh, ''Changes in American Electoral Turnout, 1965–1976,'' a paper delivered at the Annual Meeting of the Midwest Political Science Association, 1979.)

14

relatively poorly positioned in relation to turnout, have fallen even further behind. The result is an electorate that has been restructured in recent years to better represent those who, in effect, require the least representation: better educated, professionally accomplished individuals with high incomes. Voters with the lowest incomes and least formal education, unskilled and blue collar workers, and minority group members, who are more in need of a direct voice in government policy, have displayed the lowest levels of involvement. In terms of political identifications, Republicans participate more than do Democrats, and independents and weak and leaning Democrats participate the least of all. Liberals and moderates vote markedly less than do conservatives. Ideologues in general (whether conservative or liberal) tend to participate at higher levels in presidential elections (although there are variations in the pattern depending on the year and the candidates). The most consistently impressive group in voter turnout would have to be the strong Republicans.

Possibly the most exhaustive study of the demography of voting and nonvoting has been done by Raymond E. Wolfinger and Steven J. Rosenstone,[3] who used 1972 and, to a more limited extent, 1974 United States Census data (weighted to represent 128,582 respondents in 1972 and 129,801 in 1974) to examine turnout among various subgroups within the population. The significance of the study is in the number of individuals involved (normally surveys interview only between 1500 and 3000 adults) and the in-depth examination of participation patterns among demographic groups. Based on these data, the authors were able to establish the voting turnout for the politically significant demographic groups in the population and the extent to which each of the groups is over- or underrepresented in the electorate (Table 2.2).[4] Column 1 in Table 2.3 represents the demographic groups' share of the total voting age population; column 2, its share of the *actual* electorate (those who voted); and column 3, the margin of difference between the proportion voting and population size. The latter measure provides a rough index of the group's representation in the electorate. Any group—women, those with 12 years of schooling, those between 25 and 36, or those earning just below $10,000—that approaches 1.00 has a turnout figure proportionate to its numbers in the population. Those above or below this figure are over- or underrepresented among actual voters.[5]

15

TABLE 2.2 ■ Percent of Voters and Nonvoters Compared on Demographic Characteristics and Party Identification, 1972

Demographic Characteristics	(1) Percent of the Adult Citizen Population[a]	(2) Percent of Voters[b]	(3) (2) − (1)	(4) (2) ÷ (1)
Years of education				
0–4	3.6	2.0	−1.5	.56
5–7	6.4	4.7	−1.7	.73
(subtotal)	36.4	29.0	−7.4	.80
8	10.0	8.8	−1.2	.88
9–11	16.4	13.5	−2.9	.82
12	37.6	38.7	1.1	1.03
1–3 college	14.2	16.8	2.6	1.18
(subtotal)	26.0	32.3	6.3	1.24
4 college	7.3	9.4	2.1	1.29
5+ college	4.5	6.1	1.6	1.36
Family income				
Under $2,000	6.2	4.3	−1.9	.69
$2,000–$7,499	34.0	29.0	−5.0	.85
(subtotal)	55.2	48.0	−7.2	.87
$7,500–$9,999	15.0	14.7	−0.3	.98
$10,000–$14,999	25.6	28.1	2.5	1.10
$15,000–$24,999	14.5	17.6	3.1	1.21
(subtotal)	19.3	23.8	4.5	1.23
$25,000 and over	4.8	6.2	1.4	1.29
Age				
18–24	17.9	14.2	−3.7	.79
25–31	14.6	13.7	−0.9	.94
(subtotal)	32.5	27.9	−4.6	.86
32–36	8.2	8.3	0.1	1.01
37–69	49.7	54.8	5.1	1.10
70–78	6.5	6.6	0.1	1.02
79 and over	3.1	2.4	−0.7	.77

Women		53.2	52.7	−0.5	.99
Unmarried or separated		30.2	26.4	−3.8	.87
Students, age 18–24		2.7	2.8	−0.1	1.04
Southerners		25.6	21.6	−4.0	.84
Government employees		10.2	12.6	2.4	1.24
Unemployed		2.7	2.2	−0.5	.81
Blacks		9.8	8.2	−1.6	.84
Puerto Ricans[c]		.6	.3	−0.3	.50
Chicanos[c]		1.9	1.3	−0.6	.68
Length of residence[c]					
less than 4 months		7.3	3.1	−3.6	.42
4–6 months		5.7	3.0	−2.7	.53
7–11 months		4.5	2.6	−1.9	.58
	33.4		20.8	−12.6	.62
1–2 years		15.9	12.1	−3.8	.76
3–5 years		16.1	16.3	0.2	1.01
6–9 years		13.5	15.8	2.3	1.17
10 or more years		37.1	46.6	9.5	1.26
Party Identification					
Strong Democrat		14.5	15.7	1.2	1.08
Weak Democrat		26.1	25.1	−1.0	.96
Independent Democrat		10.8	10.5	−0.3	.97
	51.4		51.3	−0.1	1.00
Independent		12.5	9.1	−3.4	.73
Independent Republican		10.9	11.3	0.4	1.04
Weak Republican		14.2	15.4	1.2	1.08
Strong Republican		10.9	13.0	2.1	1.19
	36.0		39.7	3.7	1.10
Total		99.9	100.1	–	–
(N)		(2246)	(1651)	–	–

Source: Raymond E. Wolfinger and Steven J. Rosenstone. *Who Votes?*, New Haven: Yale University Press, 1980. Data from U.S. Bureau of the Census and the Center for Political Studies 1972 National Election Study.

[a] Citizens over the age of 17 for whom turnout was reported.
[b] Voters in the 1972 general election.
[c] Estimated using 1974 data.

Based on these data, the demographic and political (measured in terms of party identification) groups with the greatest and the least proportionate share of the voting population are as follows:

■ Overrepresented	■ Underrepresented
College educated	Those with the least formal education
Highest income	
Middle aged and older	Lowest income
Government employees	Young (and very old)
Residentially stable	Unmarried
Strong Republicans	Southerners
	Unemployed
	Blacks
	Chicanos
	Puerto Ricans
	Residentially mobile
	Independents

The pictures presented by the various studies utilizing different data sources coincide. Participation is decreasing across the board among all demographic groups, but it is falling off the most among the young and those at the bottom of the socioeconomic scale. As a result, the electorate is increasingly skewed to represent the interests of the well-off.[6]

■■■ TURNOUT IN THE STATES

Turnout at the state level reflects national tendencies, although the patterns are more complex than one might assume (Table 2.3). Beginning in the sixties, turnout in the individual states has declined for presidential contests, congressional elections (in both off-year and presidential years), and gubernatorial elections (figures not shown).[7] Yet the rates of decline vary substantially. From 1960 to 1980, Indiana, New Hampshire, New York, Pennsylvania, Washington, West Virginia, and Wyoming—states with apparently little in common—experienced a decrease of 20 percent or better (about twice the national average) in voter turnout for presidential elections. Similarly, and for no apparent reason, three states—Illinois, Indiana, and West Virginia—have 30 percent fewer voters participating in off-year congressional elections, which is well above the norm for all of the states taken together.[8]

There is no readily agreed-on set of reasons put forward for the decrease in voter turnout nationally or in individual states. Youth, education, the Twenty-sixth Amendment, increased mobility of the population, economic recessions (which influence the withdrawal of lower socioeconomic groups), a change in voter attitudes (especially in relation to government responsiveness), the increasing role of the media, and weakening party ties have been advanced, often in contradiction of each other, to explain the decline in voter turnout. No one questions what has occurred. Few agree on the reasons for it.[9]

One thing all would agree on is that while turnout has been decreasing nationally, it has increased in the southern states (Table 2.4). In the eleven states of the Old Confederacy, participation in presidential elections has risen from an average of less than 40 percent of the voting age population in 1960 to roughly one-half by 1980. At the same time, the gap between the region's turnout and that for the country as a whole has shrunk from 25 percent to 6 percent. The southern states are approaching the national norm for participation.

The reasons for this counter-trend are not difficult to identify. The Voting Rights Act of 1965 forced the inclusion of blacks into the southern electorate, fueling the realignment in progress and directly increasing the number of eligible black voters, which has resulted in significantly higher turnouts for the region.[10] From 1960 to 1976, black registration was up in Mississippi from 5 percent to 60 percent; in Georgia, from 29 percent to 75 percent; in South Carolina and Alabama, from 14 percent to 57 and 58 percent respectively; and in Virginia, 23 percent to 55 percent. Overall, 30 percent of blacks were registered as against 64 percent of whites in 1960. By 1976, the corresponding figures were 64 percent for blacks and 69 percent for whites. In several states (Arkansas with 94 percent and Georgia with 75 percent), black voter registration substantially outdistanced that of whites, although in sheer numbers, of course, whites continued to hold the balance of power.   19

TABLE 2.3 ■ Votes in Millions Cast for President by Regions, States, and Parties, 1972–1980

Region and State	1972				1976				1980			
	Total[a]	Democratic Party	Republican Party	Percent for Leading Party	Total[a]	Democratic Party	Republican Party	Percent for Leading Party	Total[a]	Democratic Party	Republican Party	Percent for Leading Party
Total	77,719	29,170	47,170	R-60.7	81,558	40,831	39,148	D-50.1	88,515	35,484	43,904	R-50.7
Northeast	19,952	8278	11,483	R-57.6	19,520	9929	9272	D-50.9	19,206	8019	9147	R-47.6
North Central	23,190	9127	13,711	R-59.1	24,155	11,671	11,995	R-49.7	25,178	10,291	12,827	R-50.9
South	20,048	6087	13,666	R-68.2	23,198	12,520	10,394	D-54.0	25,813	11,554	13,118	R-50.8
West	14,529	5679	8309	R-57.2	14,682	6711	7488	R-51.0	16,318	5620	8813	R-54.0
Ala	1006	257	729	R-72.4	1183	659	504	D-55.7	1342	637	654	R-48.8
Alaska	95	33	55	R-58.1	124	44	72	R-57.9	158	42	86	R-54.3
Ariz	623	199	403	R-64.7	743	295	419	R-56.4	874	247	530	R-60.6
Ark	651	200	449	R-68.9	768	499	268	D-65.0	838	398	403	R-48.1
Calif	8368	3476	4602	R-55.0	7867	3742	3882	R-49.3	8587	3084	4525	R-52.7
Colo	954	330	597	R-62.6	1082	460	584	R-54.0	1184	368	652	R-55.1
Conn	1384	555	811	R-58.6	1382	648	719	R-52.1	1106	542	677	R-48.2
Del	236	92	140	R-59.6	236	123	110	D-52.0	236	106	111	R-47.2
D.C.	163	128	35	D-78.1	169	138	28	D-81.6	175	131	24	D-74.8
Fla	2583	718	1858	R-71.9	3151	1636	1470	D-51.9	3687	1419	2047	R-55.5
Ga	1175	290	881	R-75.0	1467	979	484	D-66.7	1597	891	654	D-55.8
Hawaii	270	101	169	R-62.5	291	147	140	D-50.6	303	136	130	D-44.8
Idaho	310	81	199	R-64.2	344	127	204	R-59.3	437	110	291	R-66.5
Ill	4723	1913	2788	R-59.0	4719	2271	2364	R-50.1	4750	1981	2358	R-49.6
Ind	2126	709	1405	R-66.1	2220	1015	1184	R-53.3	2242	844	1256	R-56.0
Iowa	1226	496	706	R-57.6	1279	620	633	R-49.5	1318	509	676	R-51.3
Kans	916	270	620	R-67.7	958	430	503	R-52.5	980	326	587	R-57.9
Ky	1067	371	676	R-63.4	1167	616	532	D-52.8	1295	616	635	R-49.1
La	1051	298	687	R-65.3	1278	661	587	D-51.7	1549	708	793	R-51.2
Maine	417	161	256	R-61.5	483	232	236	R-48.9	523	221	239	R-45.6
Md	1354	506	829	R-61.3	1440	760	673	D-52.8	1540	726	681	D-47.1

State												
Mass	2459	1333	1112	D-54.2	2548	1429	1030	D-56.1	2524	1054	1058	R-41.9
Mich	3490	1459	1962	R-56.2	3654	1697	1894	R-51.8	3910	1662	1915	R-49.0
Minn	1742	802	898	R-51.6	1950	1070	819	R-54.9	2052	954	873	D-46.5
Miss	646	127	505	R-78.2	769	381	367	D-49.6	893	429	441	R-49.4
Mo	1856	697	1154	R-62.2	1954	998	927	D-51.1	2100	931	1074	R-51.2
Mont	318	120	184	R-57.9	329	149	174	R-52.8	364	118	207	R-56.8
Nebr	576	170	406	R-70.5	608	234	360	R-59.2	641	167	420	R-65.5
Nev	182	66	116	R-63.7	202	92	101	R-50.2	248	67	155	R-62.5
N.H.	334	116	214	R-64.0	340	148	186	R-54.7	384	109	222	R-57.7
N.J.	2997	1102	1846	R-61.6	3014	1445	1510	R-50.1	2976	1147	1547	R-52.0
N. Mex	386	141	236	R-61.0	418	201	211	R-50.5	457	168	251	R-54.9
N.Y.	7166	2951	4193	R-58.5	6534	3390	3101	D-51.9	6202	2728	2894	R-46.7
N.C.	1519	439	1055	R-69.5	1679	927	742	D-55.2	1856	876	915	R-49.3
N. Dak	281	100	174	R-62.1	297	135	153	R-51.6	302	79	194	R-64.2
Ohio	4095	1559	2442	R-59.6	4112	2012	2001	D-48.9	4284	1752	2207	R-51.5
Okla	1030	247	759	R-73.7	1092	532	546	R-50.0	1150	402	695	R-60.5
Oreg	928	393	487	R-52.4	1030	490	492	R-47.8	1182	457	571	R-48.3
Pa	4592	1797	2715	R-59.1	4621	2329	2206	D-50.4	4562	1938	2262	R-49.6
R.I.	416	195	220	R-53.0	411	228	181	D-55.4	416	198	155	D-47.7
S.C.	674	187	477	R-70.8	803	451	346	D-56.2	894	430	442	R-49.4
S. Dak	307	140	166	R-54.2	301	147	152	R-50.4	328	104	198	R-60.5
Tenn	1201	357	813	R-67.7	1476	826	634	R-55.9	1618	783	788	R-48.7
Tex	3471	1154	2299	R-66.2	4072	2082	1953	D-51.1	4542	1881	2511	R-55.3
Utah	478	126	324	R-67.6	541	182	338	R-62.4	604	124	440	R-72.8
Vt	187	68	117	R-62.7	188	81	102	R-54.4	213	82	95	R-44.4
Va	1457	439	988	R-67.8	1697	814	837	R-49.3	1866	752	990	R-53.0
Wash	1471	568	837	R-56.9	1558	717	778	R-50.0	1742	650	865	R-49.7
W. Va	762	277	485	R-63.6	751	436	315	D-58.0	738	367	334	D-49.8
Wis	1853	810	989	R-53.4	2104	1040	1005	D-49.4	2273	982	1089	R-47.9
Wyo	148	44	100	R-69.0	156	62	93	R-59.3	177	49	111	R-62.6

Source: U.S. Department of Commerce, Bureau of the Census, *Statistical Abstract of the United States, 1981.*
a Includes other parties.

TABLE 2.4 ■ Percent of Voter Turnout in Presidential Elections in the South and in the Nation, 1960–1980

	1960	1964	1968	1972	1976	1980
South	38.9	44.3	50.8	44.7	47.5	49.5
U.S.	63.7	62.9	61.8	55.7	54.4	55.7
Difference	−24.8	−18.6	−11.0	−11.0	−6.9	−6.2

Source: U.S. Bureau of the Census.

Harold W. Stanley has shown the results of those registration changes (Table 2.5).[11] Extrapolating from survey data provided by the Center for Political Studies, Stanley estimates the increase in black turnout from about 11 percent in 1952 to 65 percent in 1980, the latter figure rivaling the 68 percent white turnout in the region (as estimated by survey data). In a study of black political participation in Alabama, Jeffrey E. Cohen, Patrick R. Cotter, and Philip B. Coulter report that not only is black voting up but "blacks now participate at a rate higher than their social status positions would indicate." They argue that this "overparticipation," as they call it, "is due to the quality of black leadership in the South, the linkage of personal and public problems, and a sense

TABLE 2.5 ■ Southern Presidential Turnout by Race, Ten–State South, 1952–1980

Year	White[a] Turnout (%)	(N)	Black Turnout (%)	(N)	Number of Voters (in millions) White	Black	Absolute Increase Since 1952 (in millions) White	Black
1952	60.3	(252)	11.0	(91)	7.2	0.5		
1956	63.3	(341)	15.0	(80)	7.3	0.4	0.1	−0.1
1960	73.4	(391)	25.4	(67)	8.7	0.5	1.5	0.1
1964	66.9	(735)	51.0	(186)	9.4	1.8	2.2	1.3
1968	69.5	(524)	63.4	(112)	11.3	2.2	4.2	1.7
1972	61.2	(456)	59.2	(125)	11.2	3.0	4.1	2.5
1976	64.1	(455)	58.2	(125)	13.5	3.4	6.3	2.9
1980	68.4	(320)	65.0	(60)	17.6	2.8	10.4	2.8

Source: Harold W. Stanley, "The Political Impact of Electoral Mobilization: The South and Universal Suffrage, 1952–1980," a paper delivered at the Annual Meeting of the American Political Science Association, New York, 1981.
[a] The number of voters by race is estimated by assuming that the relative racial shares of the voters revealed in the surveys hold for voters in the aggregate.

of purposiveness for black political action."[12] If true, these may be among the qualities lacking in elections nationwide.

CONCLUSION

It could be argued that the proportionate importance of a group in the electorate, measured by their voter turnout, directly relates to the policy and the more generalized political rewards group members can expect from those in elective office. Obviously, many factors influence any distribution of rewards, but the general point seems defensible. If so, the restructuring of the electorate toward upper socioeconomic groups limits the representation of exactly those elements in society most in need of it.

A second argument has been made concerning low-turnout elections that appears particularly appropriate in the contemporary setting. It has been contended that contests with a low level of voter participation are more vulnerable to control by single issue groups and other political action committees (PACs). The belief is that a single issue group that can guarantee its favored candidate a vote of 5 to 10 percent of the total turnout (which may be only one-fifth to one-third of the voting age population) has enormous bargaining power, strong enough in fact to swing the election to their candidate. The threat of such group voting in a congressional or primary election has often been sufficient in recent contests to persuade both candidates to publicly commit themselves to the single issue group's policy position (on abortion, for example).[13]

We conclude with questions. Is it reasonable to accept E. E. Schattschneider's notion of "implied consent" and assume that those who do not vote are satisfied with the system and their place in the social order?[14] If so, then levels of voter participation per se are of no particular concern (and, in fact, the real threat may be from a large voter turnout that, so the theory goes, could introduce elements of instability and volatility into election outcomes). If noninvolvement masks a frustration and dissatisfaction with politics, governing institutions, and contemporary conditions in general, then there could be problems involving, to different degrees, a rejection of the system and undercutting the institutional legitimacy of political decision-making. "Implied consent" could be a disarming but potentially dangerous assumption.

If fewer and fewer voters participate, if distrust, cynicism, and alienation are on the increase, and if political institutions appear to be held in disrepute by large numbers of people, one has to wonder where the political system is headed. It may be that the pathologies presented are symptomatic of a political (and party) system in transition. If so, the question becomes transition toward *what*.

It could be argued that the present trends represent cyclical, and not very significant, variations in turnout. This assumption could lead one to dismiss them or to seek manageable, concrete solutions to the problems that are minimally disruptive to the system. It appears such a conforting approach will not work. "The evidence," says Walter Dean Burnham, "is pretty overwhelming that the current low levels of participation correspond no longer, as they did in the 1900–1930 era, to sudden inflations of the eligible population base, or to the piling up of procedural barriers designed to discourage participation by the lower order. They correspond instead to a degeneration, now very far advanced, in the collective structures of electoral politics: in short, to the degeneration of the political parties."[15] There are no ready solutions. One way or another, the problems will be with us for a long time to come.

CHAPTER 3

THE NATURE OF PARTY COMPETITION

■■

America has a functioning two-party system, which is a rarity. Depending on the weight given third-party successes, basically only British Commonwealth countries would enter any discussion of two-party or modified two-party systems. The only "pure" two-party system may exist in the United States.

■■■■ TWO-PARTY COMPETITION OVER TIME

An examination of presidential elections over several generations (Table 3.1) illustrates the relative closeness of the vote decision. Although there are fluctuations from election to election, one party or the other predominating in a given era, the parties still divide the vote and the spoils of office fairly evenly.

Much the same pattern is evident in Congressional elections (United States House of Representatives returns) where, if anything, the competition may be more consistent (Table 3.2). Many analysts consider Congressional elections to be a more valid indication of the party vote and the partisan division in the electorate since they are free of many of the issue and personality factors that can introduce short-term fluctuations into presidential contests.

Charles Sellers, examining the division of the presidential and the House vote from the creation of the party system to the mod-

TABLE 3.1 ■ Division of the Vote for Presidential Elections, 1920–1980

Year	Republicans (%)	Democrats (%)
1980	55.3	44.7
1976	48.9	51.1
1972	61.8	38.2
1968	50.4	49.6
1964	38.6	61.4
1960	49.9	50.1
1956	59.3	40.7
1952	55.7	44.3
1948	47.8	52.2
1944	46.2	53.8
1940	44.9	55.1
1936	37.5	62.5
1932	40.9	59.1
1928	58.3	41.7
1924	65.1	34.9
1920	64.0	36.0

ern era (1789–1960), has speculated that there is an internal dynamism to competitive patterns—an "equilibrium" mechanism—that produces an extraordinary stability within the system. Party strength, he believes, fluctuates only minimally over a series of elections, barring any critical realignments that would dramatically and permanently reshape party alignments (as, for example, in the period 1928–1936).[1]

Most elections fall within or close to a "normal" range of +5 to −5 percent of an equal division of the vote. Even when one party does establish a substantial advantage over the opposition in one election or over a series of elections—the Democratic dominance of 1800–1828 and from 1932 to the present, and the Republican one-partyism of 1860–1876 and 1896–1928—there is a gradual but persistent return to a two-party equilibrium. Even during these periods of one-party dominance, the opposition can win control of the presidency or the Congress based on short-term factors that work to its advantage.

The more important finding is the continued easing toward a competitive balance. Sellers puts this down to the pluralistic nature of American society. There are so many religious, economic, occupational, social, ethnic, regional, and ideological groupings within the electorate, all making their own demands on government and all with different policy objectives, that in effect an impossible overload on political decision-making is cre-

TABLE 3.2 ■ Division of the Vote for Congressional Elections, 1920–1982

Year	Republicans (%)	Democrats (%)	Year	Republicans (%)	Democrats (%)
1982	42.7	57.3	1950	50.0	50.0
1980	49.7	50.3	1948	46.7	53.3
1978	45.7	54.3	1946	54.5	45.5
1976	42.8	57.2	1944	47.7	52.3
1974	41.2	58.8	1942	51.9	48.1
1972	47.3	52.7	1940	46.7	53.3
1970	45.2	54.8	1938	48.6	51.4
1968	49.2	50.8	1936	41.5	58.5
1966	49.1	50.9	1934	45.2	54.8
1964	41.8	58.2	1932	44.4	55.6
1962	48.0	52.0	1930	54.2	45.8
1960	46.0	54.0	1928	57.6	42.4
1958	44.4	55.6	1926	60.0	40.0
1956	48.3	51.7	1924	60.0	40.0
1954	47.6	52.4	1922	55.5	44.5
1952	49.1	50.9	1920	62.5	37.5

Source: Bureau of the Census.

ated. The parties—in a one-party era—cannot satisfactorily reward the groups in their coalitions. The larger the coalition, the greater both the expectations and the number of groups demanding satisfaction. Hence, the greater the dominance of one party, the greater the likelihood that it will not meet the needs of the coalition.

As a consequence, the party loyalty of the less favored is severely tested. They tend to break away from the ruling coalition, returning to their party of original identification, or they gravitate to the opposition party if it can convince them that it will make an effort in the future to represent their concerns.

This process can be gradual, a so-called secular realignment, involving a modest but cumulative shift toward the opposition from one election to the next. Blacks are given as one example of this movement. Long considered a Republican vote in the aftermath of the Civil War and the Lincoln heritage, their party loyalty was tested by the economic policies of Franklin Roosevelt and the New Deal. These economic inducements to support Democratic policies in turn were reinforced by the civil rights initiatives and social policies of the Kennedy-Johnson years. As a result, what began as a trickle of black support for the Democrats eventually turned into a flood. By the late sixties and continuing to the eighties, black voters constituted the largest and most consistently loyal block (with the possible exception of Jewish voters) within the Democratic coalition.

Catholic voters have often been put forward as an example of a secular realignment favoring the Republicans. Based on ethnic and urban ties to the machine, Catholics were strong Democratic supporters. As Catholics climbed the socioeconomic ladder and moved from the cities to the suburbs, their voting habits changed. When analyzed by economic status and on measures of support for lifestyle issues, Catholics have increased the proportionate share of the vote they give Republicans (although not nearly as dramaticly as have blacks).[2]

The second process of change involves the "critical" election or critical election period that leads to an immediate realignment, an abrupt and permanent change in the party division of the vote. The New Deal era has already been presented as an example of this type of critical realignment. The elections of 1860 and 1896 also produced dramatic realignments, the 1890s reestablishing the supremacy of the Republicans, rather than creating a newly dominant opposition party. The changes in attitude produced by the

1964 election would seem to indicate that ideology has begun to polarize the parties. One of the bones of contention regarding electoral behavior in recent years has been whether another realignment has taken place, is taking place, or will take place.[3]

American parties are certainly in a period of destabilization. Party loyalties have weakened, there is a shifting group pattern to the vote, and election outcomes from one election to the next can, and do, swing wildly and unpredictably. These are all signs of a deinstitutionalization that could lead in time to a new alignment and a new party period.[4]

■■■ TWO-PARTY COMPETITION: ILLUSION OR FACT

Without question, America has a two-party system at the national level. However, the actual extent of two-partyism is deceptive. There are pockets of one-party dominance or of no-party competition that are more common than an examination of the national level vote returns indicates.

As previously mentioned, there have been, periods of one-party dominance during different historical eras. These are easily identified, but given the eventual return of the system to competitive status, or the emergence of the second party as the principal force in elections, the national trends do not necessarily rebut the Sellers argument on equilibrium. Still, there is more to the story.

Congressional races are a good example and are considerably less competitive than they appear. First, the vote in an election does not necessarily dictate the representative edge one party receives. Institutional factors introduce a systematic bias into outcomes. For example, Democratic House candidates averaged 54 percent of the vote in the six House election held in the period 1970–1980, but managed to control 61 percent of the seats in the Congress. In several elections, the discrepancy between the popular vote won and the proportion of seats captured in the House exceeded 10 percentage points.[5]

The discrepancy is not accidental. In part, it comes from the domimant party's ability to control the redistricting processes at the state level. With reapportionment taking place after each decennial census, the party that controls the majority of state legislatures can provide itself with a substantial edge in representation, and one that does not show up on measures based on vote totals.

A second point is more philosophical or, depending on your commitments, definitional. For many, a competitive process means the alternate sharing of power. Yet, while the vote totals of the two parties are close, the Republicans have only controlled both houses of the Congress twice (1946–1948 and 1952–1954) and the U.S. Senate one additional time (1980 to time of this writing) in the post-World War II era.

Again, when other aspects of the congressional vote are examined more intensively, the nature of competition becomes more problematic. Incumbents are seldom defeated. In the decade between 1970 and 1980, 93 percent of incumbents who sought reelection won offices. Those seeking reelection constituted an average of 83 percent of the House membership.[6] Most incumbent congressmen seek reelection and, of those who do, virtually all win. A close division of the general election vote does not reflect this monopolization of office by incumbents.

The actual turnover in seats from one Congress to the next is small. The number of seats changing from one party's control to the other's is even smaller. An examination of the incumbents defeated by members of the opposition party since the fifties shows an average of between 10 and 15 seats per election moving from the control of one party to the other.[7] Most of the total is explained by a handful of elections. Republican Congressional seats won in the Eisenhower victory of 1952 were lost in 1954. The Eisenhower recession of 1958 lost his party thirty-five seats, two-thirds of which the Republicans regained in 1960. The Goldwater debacle cost the Republicans thirty-nine Congressional seats in 1964, but two years later, the Republicans recaptured the same number they had lost. The Watergate crisis of 1972–1973 and the Nixon resignation hurt the party as well. Thirty-six seats were lost in the off-year election of 1974, then in 1980, the Republicans showed a net gain of twenty-four seats in the House. In 1982, the party lost twenty-six seats to the Democrats. It appears to take an event of some magnitude to force a change of consequence in the number of incumbent seats switching between the political parties. The normal give-and-take of electioneering appears not to offer this opportunity.

The insulation of Congressional representatives from all but the most threatening of political tides is apparent when the number of "safe" seats in recent elections (a "safe" seat is one won by an incumbent with 60 percent or more of the vote) is examined. Between 1970 and 1980, the number of safe seats in the House averaged three out of four of all of those contested. Compared with the fifties, such races are becoming more common.[8] Noncompetition is becoming the norm.

Noncompetition is found at other levels also. Nonpartisan races are actually legally mandated in many localities[9] and two states, Minnesota (up until 1974) and Nebraska (to this day) have held (or hold) nonpartisan state legislative contests. Individual races within states can be noncompetitive, either by tradition, because of the political characteristics of the electoral unit, or through the powers of incumbency. They can range from United States Senate and gubernatorial contests on down to sheriff, county commission, and school district races. In fact, competition increases with the visibility of the race.

The most competitive races are the presidential and gubernatorial contests, the least competitive, the local contests. The experience with House seats applies elsewhere.

Finally, some states or regions exhibit consistent patterns of one-party support. Kansas is Republican, Massachusetts Democratic. For long periods, the Midwest, the Plains States, and upper New England were one-party Republican, the South one-party Democratic. Even today, although much is heard about the "southern strategies" of the Republican party and the resurgence of two-party competition in the region, most races below the presidential level in the South are decisively Democratic.[10]

One explanation for the erratic competitive patterns in the nation and the consistent lack of serious competition in certain areas, in most local races, and in races for different types of elective office is put forward by Walter Dean Burnham. Basically, Burnham argues that the failure of the New Deal realignment—an incomplete revolution—to totally mobilize the population into contrasting political (and social) camps has had continuing relevance for each level of American politics. Burnham puts it this way:

> . . . an extremely important factor in the recent
> evolution of the voting universe has been the extent
> to which the imperatives of the class-ethnic New Deal
> realignment have been relevant to the local social
> structure and political culture. In the absence of an
> effectively integrating set of state political
> organizations, issues and candidates around which a

TABLE 3.3 ■ Demographic Support for Presidential Candidates, 1952–1980

	1952		1956		1960		1964	
	Stevenson (%)	Ike (%)	Stevenson (%)	Ike (%)	JFK (%)	Nixon (%)	LBJ (%)	Goldwater (%)
National	44.6	55.4	42.2	57.8	50.1	49.9	61.3	38.7
Sex								
Male	47	53	45	55	52	48	60	40
Female	42	58	39	61	49	51	62	38
Race								
White	43	57	41	59	49	51	59	41
Nonwhite	79	21	61	39	68	32	94	6
Education								
College	34	66	31	69	39	61	52	48
High school	45	55	42	58	52	48	62	38
Grade school	52	48	50	50	55	45	66	34
Occupation								
Prof. & business	36	64	32	68	42	58	54	46
White collar	40	60	37	63	48	52	57	43
Manual	55	45	50	50	60	40	71	29
Age								
Under 30 years	51	49	43	57	54	46	64	36
30–49 years	47	53	45	55	54	46	63	37
50 years & older	39	61	39	61	46	54	59	41
Religion								
Protestants	37	63	37	63	38	62	55	45
Catholics	56	44	51	49	78	22	76	24
Politics								
Republicans	8	92	4	96	5	95	20	80
Democrats	77	23	85	15	84	16	87	13
Independents	35	65	30	70	43	57	56	44
Region								
East	45	55	40	60	53	47	68	32
Midwest	42	58	41	59	48	52	61	39
South	51	49	49	51	51	49	52	48
West	42	58	43	57	49	51	60	40
Members of Labor Union Families	61	39	57	43	65	35	73	27

TABLE 3.3 ■ Continued

	1968			1972		1976[b]			1980		
	HHH (%)	Nixon (%)	Wallace (%)	McGovern (%)	Nixon (%)	Carter (%)	Ford (%)	McCarthy (%)	Carter (%)	Reagan (%)	Anderson (%)
National	43.0	43.4	13.6	38	62	50	48	1	41	51	7
Sex											
Male	41	43	16	37	63	53	45	1	38	53	7
Female	45	43	12	38	62	48	51	a	44	49	6
Race											
White	38	47	15	32	68	46	52	1	36	56	7
Nonwhite	85	12	3	87	13	85	15	a	86	10	2
Education											
College	37	54	9	37	63	42	55	2	35	53	10
High school	42	43	15	34	66	54	46	a	43	51	5
Grade school	52	33	15	49	51	58	41	1	54	42	3
Occupation											
Prof. & business	34	56	10	31	69	42	56	1	33	55	10
White collar	41	47	12	36	64	50	48	2	40	51	9
Manual	50	35	15	43	57	58	41	1	48	46	5
Age											
Under 30 years	47	38	15	48	52	53	45	1	47	41	11
30–49 years	44	41	15	33	67	48	49	2	38	52	8
50 years & older	41	47	12	36	64	52	48	a	41	54	4
Religion											
Protestants	35	49	16	30	70	46	53	a	39	54	6
Catholics	59	33	8	48	52	57	42	1	46	47	6
Politics											
Republicans	9	86	5	5	95	9	91	a	8	86	5
Democrats	74	12	14	67	33	82	18	a	69	26	4
Independents	31	44	25	31	69	38	57	4	29	55	14
Region											
East	50	43	7	42	58	51	47	1	43	47	9
Midwest	44	47	9	40	60	48	50	1	41	51	7
South	31	36	33	29	71	54	45	a	44	52	3
West	44	49	7	41	59	46	51	1	35	54	9
Members of Labor Union Families	56	29	15	46	54	63	36	1	50	43	5

Source: Various Public Opinion Poll Survey Data (Gallup Poll) as reported in *The Gallup Report*.
[a] Less than one percent.
[b] Results for 1976 and 1980 do not include vote for minor party candidates.

> relatively intense polarization of voters can develop,
> politics is likely to have so little salience that very
> substantial portions of the potential electorate either
> exclude themselves altogether from the political
> system or enter it in an erratic and occasional way. As
> organized and articulated in political terms, the
> contest between "business" and "government" which
> has tended to be the linchpin of our national politics
> since the 1930s has obviously made no impression
> upon many in the lowest income strata of the urban
> population. It has also failed among local political
> cultures which remain largely pre-industrial in
> outlook and social structure.[11]

Burnham is discussing participation specifically, but the same structural forces within the society that he refers to would work to depress the relevance—and hence the intensity and comprehensiveness—of competitive patterns at all levels as well. Whatever the underlying causes, party competitive patterns are erratic at best, something less than the top to bottom struggle between two well-matched coalitions.

The United States can claim a competitive two-party system, but the overall indicators of competition can and do hide pockets of noncompetition, of which the House races are indicative. These pockets do have the advantage of insuring predictable and continuing party support. Nonetheless, the problems may outweigh the advantages. A lack of consistent competition is evident at most levels, a condition that raises questions about the accountability and responsiveness of a party system that theoretically offers a choice between two alternatives.

■■■ THE DEMOGRAPHIC COMPONENTS OF PARTY COMPETITION

Party competition is built on the shifting loyalties of the social groups that comprise an extremely heterogeneous and constantly fluctuating electorate. Demographic groups have distinct tendencies to consistently support one party or the other over time. However, a swing of several percentage points in group support patterns or a lessened tendency among group members to vote with the same intensity for the normally preferred party can provide the margin of victory for a candidate in any given election. The process can be illustrated.

Table 3.3 traces the two-party division of the vote between the parties from 1952 through 1980. The stratification (by age, income, religion, place of residence, and occupation) is immediately evident as is the variation in intensity of support for the two parties in the presidential elections. In terms of coalitional blocs, the demographic groups most pronouncedly pro-Democratic and pro-Republican are as follows:

■ Pro-Democratic	■ Pro-Republican
younger voters	older voters
those with less education	the better educated
city dwellers	those living in suburban and rural areas
lower income	those with the highest incomes
blacks	whites
members of union households	members of non-union households
blue collar and unskilled workers	professional and white collar workers
Jews	Protestants

There is then a polarization to group support patterns and a pluralism that well serves the parties and the needs of party competition. Both parties have a core support that remains loyal in election after election and gives them a stable base for competing in any individual contest or in a series of elections over any period of time. Between the most ardent loyalists, there exists a large number of intermediate groupings whose support—a few points in this direction, a few points in that—can swing elections from one party to the other. The fluctuations need not be pronounced to have a decisive impact on an election's outcome. Among the swing groups are the middle aged, the middle income earners, those with a high school education, suburbanites, and Catholics. These groups of course represent tendencies. Groups fluctuate in the extent of their support from one election to the next, depending on the candidates, the issues, and the nature of the political climate in which the election takes place.

35

Union members and their families, central city dwellers, younger voters, those with less education, and, most pronouncedly, blacks and Jews have demonstrated a decided preference for the Democratic party regardless of the election. Basically, a mirror image is evident among those social groups most loyal to the Republican party. Occasionally, there are deviations. The Catholic vote went Republican in 1956 and 1972, yet was strongly Democratic both in 1960 (when a Catholic ran for president) and in 1964.

The majority of unskilled laborers, normally heavily Democratic, voted Republican in 1972 and split its vote between the parties in 1956. In 1980, it came close to an even division again. Members of union households, a core constituency in the Democratic coalition, crossed party lines and voted Republican in 1972. The college educated, and professional, business, and white collar groups more generally, considered staples of Republican coalition, have been voting Democratic in larger numbers. These reorientations of allegiances could represent specific responses to individual elections or they could indicate the beginning of a graduated secular realignment that will reshape the parties' coalitions.[12]

More common, and of more significance for explaining immediate election outcomes, is the correlation between demographic groups in their party support patterns. While the margin of support for each of the parties among group members (high, middle, and low income earners, whites and blacks, city and suburb dwellers, and so on) remains essentially the same, the intensity of support for a party varies significantly by election. Voters of all educational backgrounds showed Republican tendencies in the fifties and in 1972, but shifted toward the Democrats in 1964, 1976, and 1960. Young and old, high and low income earners, union members and non-union members, Protestants, Jews and Catholics, and those of different occupations (with a few exceptions) moved in rhythm with the national party trends, fluctuating toward one party in one election and the other later on. This rise and fall in the intensity of support—while the magnitude of the difference remains basically the same—determines the outcome of elections and contributes directly to the highly competitive nature of the party system at the national level. With less oscillation, the same broad pattern would be repeated at other levels.

Table 3.3 can be used to examine the change in the margin of group support between 1976 and 1980. The presidential election of 1976 was basically a "dead heat." Democratic candidate Jimmy

Carter narrowly defeated incumbent Republican Gerald E. Ford with 51.05 percent of the popular vote to Ford's 48.95 percent. Four years later, the election was a landslide. Republican challenger Ronald Reagan received 51.6 percent of the popular vote to Carter's 41.7 percent.

Taken by category, the pattern becomes clear. In many respects, Reagan did not do substantially better than Ford in attracting group support. The story of the election is in the erosion of Carter's vote. It fell off 15 percent among men, 10 percent among whites, 7 to 11 percent among those attending high school and college, 10 percent among the occupation groups sampled, 10 percent or better among those over 30, 11 percent among Catholics, and 13 percent among union families. Carter's support among Democrats sank from 62 to 69 percent. The defectors from the Carter coalition marginally increased Reagan's support among most of the groups and provided the basis for the John Anderson third-party candidacy. Nonetheless, Reagan had enough appeal to traditional Democratic constituencies (blue collar workers, those with less education) to weaken Carter's vote, and this coupled with his appeal to swing groups (white southerners, Catholics, middle income voters, and those with high school or some college education) and the temptation of the Anderson appeal proved enough to give Reagan a decisive electoral victory. Oscillations among groups—while often not of great magnitude in themselves—are sufficient to keep the parties competitive at the national level.

The demographic composition of the party coalitions provides stability—there is a core vote both parties can count on—and yet allows for change and flexibility within the party system. A rise or drop of a few points in the intensity of a group's support between elections can provide the margin of victory or defeat for a party. The result is a competitive party system with both parties given the chance to win elections and control public office.

CHAPTER 4

THIRD PARTIES AND THEIR CONTRIBUTIONS TO THE PARTY SYSTEM

■■

T hird parties of any consequence occur infrequently and their impact on the political system is minimal. In fact, it is argued that third parties have only had an impact during times of crisis.

■■■ THIRD PARTIES IN HISTORY

Only eleven third parties have received more than 5.6 percent of the total popular vote, the mean vote for third party candidacies (Table 4.1). These are as follows:[1]

- Anti-Mason party, 1832. An egalitarian or extremist party, depending on the commentator, that opposed Masonry, secrecy, and religious fundamentalism in politics. The party's most notable accomplishment was the introduction in 1831 of the national convention to nominate party candidates, a device copied by the major parties and one that has survived with remarkably little change.

- Free Soil party, 1848. The first of four (five, if you count the Republicans) parties to deal with the slavery issue and the irreconcilable tensions it introduced into American life. The Free Soilers, an amalgam of a number of antislavery factions, wanted slavery restricted in the Union (at a time when neither of the major parties took a clear stand on this issue) and prohibited in the territories taken from Mexico.

- American, or Know-Nothing, party, 1856. A nativist, secret party, whose southern wing was also antiabolitionist and antislavery, it was organized to render the foreign-born population politically powerless through strict naturalization laws; it was popularly known as the Know-Nothing party because members replied "I don't know" to any questions asked in reference to the party.

- Breckinridge Democrats, 1860. When the Democratic party split over the slavery issue in 1860 (the northern wing nominating Stephen Douglas), the proslavery southern wing ran Kentuckian John C. Breckinridge on a platform advocating federal protection for "property rights" (which was intended to include slaves).

- Constitutional Union party, 1860. A centrist party whose appeal was mainly to the border and upper southern states, its candidate, John Bell of Tennessee, campaigned mainly for the preservation of the Union and the Constitution.

- Populist, or People's, party, 1892. A radical agrarian party whose members felt the major parties were captives of the eastern industrial establishment, the Populists advocated banking and land reforms, expansion of the money supply, government cooperatives, and nationalization of the means of transportation (especially railroads).

- "Bull Moose" (Teddy Roosevelt) Progressives, 1912. A party that emerged from the factional divisions within the dominant Republican party between the "old guard" William Howard Taft conservative wing and the reform wing headed by Theodore Roosevelt. When Roosevelt was denied nomination by the stage-managed 1912 Republican National Convention, he bolted the party, created the Bull Moose Progressives, and campaigned on a platform calling for the regulation of corporate enterprises and more direct democracy in politics. Roosevelt's Progressives proved to be the most electorally successful third party in history. They defeated the Republicans (who received 23.2 percent of the vote to the Progressives' 27.4 percent). This split in Republican 39 ranks is generally credited with allowing Woodrow Wilson and the Democrats to win the presidency.

- Socialist party, 1912. An anticapitalist party long under the leadership of Eugene V. Debbs, it received its largest share of the vote in the 1912 election.

- La Follette Progressives, 1924. The Progressives—a coalition of farm and urban labor with support from the A.F.L.—ran on an anticorporation, antimonopoly, return-government-to-the-people platform. Since they weren't sharing in the prosperity of the twenties, they were opposed to the business favoritism and corruption of the Republicans, feeling as well that the Democratic presidential candidate John W. Davis, a lawyer for J. P. Morgan, offered no alternative to Calvin Coolidge. The movement collapsed as a result of the death of Robert "Fighting Bob" La Follette in 1925 and the decision of the Democratic National Convention in 1928 to nominate Al Smith—a Catholic and a representative of the party's urban base—to oppose the Republicans.

- George Wallace American Independent Party, 1968. A regional southern party with some support among northern industrial workers, its candidate, segregationist George Wallace—claiming there wasn't "a dime's worth of difference" between the major parties—ran on a law-and-order, pro-Vietnam War platform that, conversely, was antistudent, antidemonstrator, antigovernment and anti-civil rights, a position that was to have echoes in the Republican campaigns of the seventies and eighties.

- John Anderson National Unity Campaign, 1980. A centrist coalition of moderate Republicans and liberal Democrats dissatisfied with the Carter administration's social policies, the Anderson campaign attempted to capitalize on the major parties' nomination of two unpopular candidates: Carter's presidency was unpopular even among Democrats and Reagan was perceived as a right-wing extremist. Anderson launched his campaign after failing to receive significant support in the Republican primaries.

The number of third parties to gain a significant following is extremely small. It is less than the number of third or minor parties that contested elections in the 1980 presidential year alone

TABLE 4.1 ■ Major Third Parties in American History[a]

Party	Year	Percent of Vote
Anti-Mason	1832	8.0
Free Soil	1848	10.1
American ("Know-Nothing")	1856	21.4
Beckinridge Democrats	1860	18.2
Constitutional Union	1860	12.6
Populists	1892	8.5
Bull Moose (Teddy Roosevelt) Progressives	1912	27.4
Socialists	1912	6.0
Robert ("Fighting Bob") La Follette Progressives	1924	16.6
George Wallace American Independent	1948	13.5
John Anderson National Unity	1980	6.6

Source: Daniel A. Mazmanian, *Third Parties in Presidential Elections*, The Brookings Institution, 1974. Data are from *Statistical Abstract of the United States*, U.S. Department of Commerce, Bureau of the Census.
[a] Third Parties receiving more than 5.6% Mazmanian calculated as the mean vote for all third parties historically.

(Table 4.2). Yet the number of these third and minor parties contesting for office is substantial. Even in off-year elections, third parties continue to seek their place in the sun. For example, in the off-year election of 1982 in New York—a state more receptive than most to third party candidacies—ten party slates were put forward for the offices of governor and lieutenant governor (Figure 4.1). Four of the parties (in addition to the Democrats and Republicans) contested for several other state offices and three of the parties fielded candidates for offices down to the local level. Nonetheless, the odds against any non–major party winning office are almost insurmountable.

■■■ THE HURDLES FACED BY THIRD PARTIES

The reasons for the third parties' lack of success are easily documented:

TABLE 4.2 ■ Parties in the 1980 Presidential Elections

Party	Number	Percent of Vote
Major Parties		
Republicans	43,893,770	50.7
Democrats	35,480,948	41.0
Third Parties		
John Anderson National	5,719,222	6.6
Unity Campaign		
Minor Parties[a]		
Libertarian	920,049	0.0106
Citizens Party	232,533	0.0026
Socialist Worker Party	48,650	0.0005624
Communist Party	43,896	0.0005074
American Independent	41,157	0.0004758
Party		
American Party	14,320	0.0001645
Workers World Party	13,213	0.0001527
National Statesman	7127	0.0000823
Party		
Socialist Party	6720	0.0000776
Peace and Freedom	18,106	0.0002093
Party		
Right to Life Party	32,319	0.0003736
Middle Class Candidate	3694	0.0000427
Party		
Down with Lawyers	1718	0.0000198
Party		
Independent Party	923	0.0000106
Natural Peoples'	296	0.0000034
League Party		

Source: *The Hammond Almanac, 1982*, Maplewood, N.J.: Hammond Almanac, Inc., 1981.
[a] Less than 5.6% of vote.

1.   Most Americans have a psychological attachment to and a record of voting for one of the two major parties. Such habits and identifications are difficult to break.

2.   Most people will vote for a third party only if it can show that it is a credible alternative, that it is capable of winning an election, that its policies are reasonable and workable, and that it will be able to govern effectively. This is virtually impossible to do in a three-month (September–November) campaign period.

3.   The third party must expend most of its time, resources, and money on simply getting on the ballot in each of the fifty states. This means meeting discriminatory election laws—

1 GOVERNOR AND LIEUTENANT-GOVERNOR (Vote ONCE)	2	3	4 COMPTROLLER (Vote for ONE)	5 ATTORNEY GENERAL (Vote for ONE)	6 UNITED STATES SENATOR (Vote for ONE)	7	8 JUSTICE OF THE SUPREME COURT (9th J.D.) (Vote for ANY FOUR)	9	10	11 Representative in Congress (22nd District) (Vote for ONE)	12 STATE SENATOR (38th District) (Vote for ONE)	13 MEMBER OF ASSEMBLY (92nd District) (Vote for ONE)	14 COUNTY JUDGE (Vote for ONE)	15 COUNTY CLERK (Vote for ONE)	16 COUNTY TREASURER (Vote for ONE)	17	18
1 A Democratic Mario M. Cuomo Alfred B. Del Bello			4 A Democratic Raymond F. Gallagher	5 A Democratic Robert Abrams	6 A Democratic Daniel P. Moynihan	7 A Democratic Lawrence N. Martin, Jr.	8 A Democratic Sondra M. Miller	9 A Democratic Ascher Katz	10 A Democratic Robert N. Kaplan	11 A Democratic Peter A. Peyser	12 A Democratic Linda Winikow	13 A Democratic Robert J. Connor	14 A Democratic Robert R. Meehan		16 A Democratic Joseph T. St.Lawrence		
1 B Republican Lew Lehrman James L. Emery			4 B Republican Edward V. Regan	5 B Republican Frances A. Sclafani	6 B Republican Florence M. Sullivan	7 B Republican Angelo J. Ingrassia	8 B Republican Louis C. Palella	9 B Republican W. Denis Donovan	10 B Republican Gerard E. Delaney	11 B Republican Benjamin A. Gilman	12 B Republican Kenneth Harfenist	13 B Republican Thomas P. Morahan	14 B Republican William F. Wray	15 B Republican Joseph R. Holland	16 B Republican Charles A. McLiverty		
1 C Conservative Lew Lehrman James L. Emery			4 C Conservative Edward V. Regan	5 C Conservative Frances A. Sclafani	6 C Conservative Florence M. Sullivan	7 C Conservative Angelo J. Ingrassia	8 C Conservative Louis C. Palella	9 C Conservative W. Denis Donovan	10 C Conservative Gerard E. Delaney	11 C Conservative Charles C. Beck	12 C Conservative Kenneth Harfenist	13 C Conservative Thomas P. Morahan	14 C Conservative William F. Wray	15 C Conservative Joseph R. Holland	16 C Conservative Charles A. McLiverty		
1 D Right to Life Robert J. Bohner Paul F. Callahan			4 D Right to Life John A. Boyle	5 D Right to Life Kevin P. McGovern	6 D Right to Life Florence M. Sullivan	7 D Right to Life Angelo J. Ingrassia	8 D Right to Life Louis C. Palella	9 D Right to Life W. Denis Donovan	10 D Right to Life Gerard E. Delaney	11 D Right to Life Richard Bruno		13 D Right to Life Thomas P. Morahan		15 D Right to Life Joseph R. Holland			
1 E Liberal Mario M. Cuomo Alfred B. Del Bello			4 E Liberal William Finneran	5 E Liberal Robert Abrams	6 E Liberal Daniel P. Moynihan	7 E Liberal Lawrence N. Martin, Jr.	8 E Liberal Sondra M. Miller	9 E Liberal Ascher Katz		11 E Liberal Peter A. Peyser	12 E Liberal Linda Winikow	13 E Liberal Robert J. Connor	14 E Liberal Robert R. Meehan		16 E Liberal Joseph T. St.Lawrence		
1 F Free Libertarian John H. Northrup David Hoesly			4 F Free Libertarian William P. McMillen	5 F Free Libertarian Dolores Grande	6 F Free Libertarian James J. McKeown												
1 G Socialist Worker Diane Wang Peter A. Thierjung					6 G Socialist Worker Steven Wattenmaker												
1 H New Alliance Nancy Ross Lenora B. Fulani																	
1 I Unity Jane Benedict Angela M. Gilliam	2 I Independent Lew Lehrman James L. Emery																

FIGURE 4.1 ■ Political parties represented on the New York State ballot, 1982.

many adopted at the turn of the century and modified since then—designed to protect the hegemony of the major parties. Such statues, which exempt the major parties from compliance, mandate high petition requirements (signed by voters not registered with either party or who have not participated in either party's primaries); a geographical apportionment to the signatures (forcing a geographical representativeness and widespread organization and working against, for example, a big city-based party); limited enrollment periods and early election year closing dates; the slating of candidates for minor state and/or for a specified number of congressional races, so that a new party's candidate is forced to organize and meet ballot requirements for a series of offices rather than concentrate on the presidency alone; the exclusion of "sore losers" (those who sought, and lost, a major party's nomination) from running. The specific statutory requirements vary by state and in each they require individual attention. The Anderson campaign spent most of its time and money contesting these provisions from the announcement of their effort in April through September of 1980. Up to the final days of the campaign, it was questionable whether Anderson—or his surrogate electors—would meet the requirements and win the court challenges necessary to appear on all fifty state ballots. One consequence of the Wallace campaign of 1968, Eugene McCarthy's independent candidate movement of 1976, and the Anderson National Unity Campaign of 1980 has been a sustained legal attack on discriminatory state party statues. A greater uniformity and simplicity to these laws has begun to emerge, which should make such challenges easier in the future.

4. A new party must field a candidate, develop a nationwide party organization, decide on and launch a media campaign, put together a coalition, construct a platform, focus on and dramatize a few major issues that will identify its campaign, attract the substantial funding necessary for campaigning (the national parties are subsidized by the federal treasury[2]), distinguish itself clearly from the major parties, and then introduce its candidates and policies and convince the public and the press that it represents a creditable alternative capable of winning the election. The two major parties, which have been doing this for over a hundred years, have difficulty in

meeting these challenges. For a new party, they constitute virtually insuperable barriers. John Anderson and his supporters had from late April until the first week in November—roughly a six month period—to accomplish these objectives.

5. The American political system stresses single member districts and plurality elections, an electoral arrangement that encourages coalitions within two broadly based and not terribly well-defined parties. A vote for a third party under such a system is normally wasted.

6. Third parties must face the accusation of being spoilers with no realistic hope of winning, their intervention serving only to force the election into the House of Representatives (if neither of the major parties gain a majority in the electoral college), with complications for the nation and the orderly transfer of power that cannot be anticipated.

7. The direct primary, introduced as part of the Progressive Movement at the turn of the century, allows all dissident elements within a party the opportunity to make themselves heard and to mobilize whatever support that exists for their policies and their candidates. It is argued that the long-run effect has been to make third-pary candidacies unnecessary.[3]

8. The media refuse to take third-party candidacies seriously or to give them the exposure needed to achieve credibility. The media, to the extent that they treat them at all, look on third parties as oddities in the national scene and deny them the access to public attention and the serious coverage a presidential candidacy would seemingly demand. In part, the media, especially television, fear the provisions of the "equal time" act and, although exclusion is made for political news, they believe that coverage of third-party activities—and especially interviews with third party candidates—could lead to demands by the nuisance parties and their nominees for similar amounts of air time. Their reservations are not ungrounded. It is a difficult problem. The candidate of the Citizens Party, Barry Commoner, a well-known environmental advocate, complained during the 1980 campaign that he received more free television time and media attention *before* he announced as a presidential candidate than after he committed himself to run.[4] In fact, once he became a presidential   45

candidate, the media became wary of him and their interest in him ceased.

The psychological, statutory, organizational, financial, and campaign barriers to a successful third-party movement appear insurmountable. And, in large part, they are. The handful of significant third-party efforts in almost two hundred years of party competition attests to how formidable the challenge is. Still, hope springs eternal. There have been rare third-party successes and, although the proposition may be debated, third parties do make a contribution to the American party system.

■■■■ THIRD PARTY IMPACT

The most notable third party in American history is, of course, the Republican party. Created in 1854 by abolitionists who believed their views were not represented by the faction-ridden Democrats and the declining Whigs, the Republicans first contested for the presidency in 1856 (finishing second in the balloting with 31 percent of the vote). Four years later, they won the presidency and since then have remained one of the nation's two major parties.

The second success of a third party involves the Populists. In 1892, their party received 8.5 percent of the vote. So in 1896, they decided to contest within the Democratic party. Their candidate (William Jennings Bryan) won the party's nomination, his platform reflecting the Populist's policy concerns and proposed solutions in a radical departure from the traditional alternatives offered by the two parties. Thus, the Democrats in the 1896 election provided a clear alternative to William McKinley and the Republicans' pro-corporate wealth platform. These developments though did not help the Democrats since the realignment brought about by the election lost them much of their urban base. A period of competitive party politics (1876–1896) was replaced by an era of one-party Republican dominance.

Paul Kleppner, in a detailed examination of the changes produced by the new coalitions,[5] has noted an immediate shift along the populous eastern seaboard and in the larger industrial states that signficantly benefited the Republicans. The West Coast also became decidedly more Republican while the plains, mountain, and border states responded more favorably to the Populist-Democratic appeal. By 1904, the Republicans had a decisive edge that gained momentum in succeeding elections. A by-product of the realignment in party coalitions and the decrease in two-party competitiveness was a major drop-off in electoral participation.

The results of these changes are hard to underestimate. Walter Dean Burnham, for example, has contended that "the structure of the American voting universe—i.e., the adult population as it exists today—was substantially formed in the period 1900–1920." Burnham continues:

> This revolutionary contraction in the size and
> diffusion in the shape of the voting universe was
> almost certainly the fruit of the heavily sectional party
> realignment which was inaugurated in 1896. This
> system of 1896 . . . led to the destruction of party
> competition throughout much of the United States,
> and thus paved the way for the rise of the direct
> primary. It also gave immense impetus to the strains
> of anti-partisan and anti-majoritarian theory and
> practice which have always been significant elements
> in the American political tradition. By the decade of
> the 1920s this new regime and business control over
> public policy in this country were consolidated. . . .
> It is difficult to avoid the impression that while all the
> forms of political democracy were more or less
> scrupulously preserved, the functional result of the
> "system of 1896" was the conversion of a fairly
> democratic regime into a rather broadly based
> oligarchy.[6]

Although Burnham's views are controversial, they do highlight the importance third parties have in affecting policy changes and in redesigning party coalitions, and, by implication, the problems a stagnant party system can develop.

■■■ THIRD PARTY CONTRIBUTIONS TO A TWO-PARTY SYSTEM

For all their faults, third parties do make a substantial contribution to the exercise of American democracy by providing an outlet for protest—and a means of gaining attention—for any segment of the population that feels neglected by the major parties and their candidates. Voting for a third party to express discontent with the two majors is a tack that has been taken by farmers, laborers, groups working against corruption in public office, and those forces that oppose elitist tendencies in government as well as excessive concentrations of wealth in the private sector. Third parties have also been used by racists, bigots, extremists, anti-civil libertarians, and religious radicals. Whatever the justness of a cause or its objectives, third parties do exist as an alternative form of protest for those whose views are not represented by either of the dominant parties.

In addition, third parties can widen the scope of major party policies by taking positions the majors consider too controversial. If these bolder positions show a potential for attracting a large voting population, then one or both the majors will adopt the issues and, with them, their public supporters. More often that not, though, when a major adopts a third-party policy, it will tailor it to meet the needs and the approval of its own coalition. Nevertheless, third-party policies that have a wide appeal can make a substantial impact on government. In his book *Third Parties in Presidential Elections*, Daniel Mazmanian discusses this point:

> . . . many of their third party's ideas have eventually been incorporated into the programs of major parties and translated into public policies. The slavery restriction and internal improvement themes of the Free Soil party of 1848 and 1852 were seized by the Republican party in 1856, and both became public policy under the Republican administrations of the 1860s. Progressive taxation, regulation of railroads, child labor laws, and social insurance were ideas introduced into the political dialogue by Socialists, Farmer-Laborites, Progressives and Populists. The major portion of the New Deal programs of Franklin Roosevelt are in some quarters attributed to the Progressive platforms of the preceding decades.
>
> Third parties have been particularly prominent in battles over suffrage and election reform. Long before such ideas were accepted by the major parties, the Populists, Progressives and Socialists were advocating the direct election of U.S. senators, women's suffrage, the recall and referendum, primary elections, and corrupt practice legislation, most of which were

enacted in the late nineteenth and early twentieth centuries.[7]

Although these contributions are impressive, Mazmanian cautions that "the connection between third-party activity and the adoption of programs is neither direct nor pervasive . . . this adoption depends on factors often beyond the control of a minority party."[8]

Despite the qualifications, whatever they may be, third-party unorthodoxy introduces a potential breeding ground for new ideas and policy departures into a party system that is not noted for the creativity of the policies it advances. The norm in this regard has been the safe, the tried, and, whether successful or not, the known. Third parties constitute a refreshing vehicle that can propose new solutions and focus on problems often ignored by the more conventional parties. A third party, unlike the major parties, has little to lose by taking bold stands.

Third, and perhaps most important of all, third parties add a flexibility that would be lacking in a strictly defined two-party system. As an alternative to a two-party system that has lost the good will of the American public and become stagnant and unresponsive to the social problems of the day, third parties offer a way out. A third party may offer new policy choices, or may focus on issues—from slavery to corporate exploitation or social injustice—that have been neglected by the major parties, or it may serve as an outlet for the anger and frustration of a reasonably large bloc of the electorate. All add to the harmony, vitality, and stability of the political system. Such services provide a welcome corrective to the cautiousness of the major parties and the limited range of issues they address. Under extreme conditions, it is possible (and it has happened) that a third party that speaks to the concerns of a nation can replace an unrepresentative and impotent major party, and in the process revitalize a tired party system and introduce a continuity in government that otherwise would be missing. It may well be that third parties, rather than being the enemy of the two-party system, provide a cushion and a degree of flexibility to the operations of the party system that has been underappreciated (contrary to a common assumption of the practitioners who have framed the statutory provisions that protect the major parties and one made by many students of political parties). If third parties did not exist, a two-party system would be well advised to invent them.

CHAPTER 5

Party Loyalty and Election Outcomes

■

arty identification has long been posited as the most forceful influence shaping the individual's vote decision, his more generalized political attitudes, and his perceptions of the political world. Party identification—a psychological measure of the long-term strength (strong, weak) and direction (Democratic, Independent, Republican) of party attachments—has been advanced as the principal factor explaining election outcomes. This is certainly true of what Philip E. Converse has referred to as the "stable party period" (1952–1964) in the contemporary cycle of elections covered by survey voting research.[1] Party identification, however, is demonstrably less important in explaining the outcomes of recent presidential elections, one indication of an electorate in flux.

Elections dominated by a long attachment to a political party were characterized by a predictability and stability to outcomes and a consistency in the party vote, from the top of the ticket to bottom, that are no longer evident. The weakening of party ties has created a volatility in election outcomes in successive years, unheard of in recent eras, and an inconsistency in party preferences and partisan advantage from one office level to the next (a measure referred to as ticket-splitting) that are difficult to predict. It is not unusual for close election outcomes in presidential contests (1960, 1968, 1976) to be interspersed with, and succeeded by, landslides (1964, 1972, 1980). The advantage to a particular party has been equally unpredictable: Democratic administrations (1960–1968)

50

have been followed by Republican administrations (1968–1976), which in turn have been followed by Democratic (1976–1980) and then again by Republican administrations (1980–). A landslide for the Democrats in 1964 was followed a few years later by a landslide in favor of the Republicans in 1972 and 1980. Ticket-splitting (not voting exclusively for one party) was rare during the fifties (averaging about 15 percent of the vote), but had more than doubled by the seventies. Congressional districts evidencing split votes (one party winning the presidential vote, the other the congressional) has increased from negligible proportions (between 3 percent and 11 percent in the years 1920–1948) to over 30 percent of all contests by the late sixties. Overall, in the past several decades, there has been a marked increase in ticket-splitting, an inconsistency in party preference, and a volatility in election performance that show no signs of abating.

▇▇▇ PARTY IDENTIFICATION

The principal reason for increasing electoral instability is the breakdown in partisan identifications. Since the measure was introduced in the early fifties to explain voter decision-making, it has remained among the most important reasons in determining the individual's vote decision and in deciphering his relationship to the political world. The identification with a party—formed early in life through family socialization processes and reinforced by time—provided an anchor for the individual's political perceptions. It also allowed analysts a degree of assurance in predicting election results in rough approximation to the partisan division of the electorate. Aberrations in outcomes (minority party victories) were viewed as short-run influences (candidate appeal, campaign issues) working to neutralize the more powerful, long-term partisan identifications. Yet these same identifications that have provided the core of the voting analyses are weakening. In recent years, they have been in systematic decline (Table 5.1).

Table 5.1 demonstrates that the proportion of partisan identifiers has been decreasing steadily. Taken by decade, partisan attachments claimed 74 percent of the voter age population in the fifties, 72 percent in the sixties and 64 percent in the seventies. Correspondingly, the proportion of the electorate that considers itself "independent" has risen from 14 percent in the fifties, to 25 percent in the sixties, and to 35 percent in the seventies. In the

TABLE 5.1 ■ Percentage of Party Identification over Time, 1952–1980

Party Identification	1952	1954	1956	1958	1960	1962	1964	1966	1968	1970	1972	1974	1976	1978	1980
Strong Democrat	22	22	21	27	20	23	27	18	20	20	15	18	15	15	17
Weak Democrat	25	26	23	22	25	23	25	28	25	24	26	21	25	24	23
Independent Democrat	10	9	6	7	6	7	9	9	10	10	11	13	12	14	11
Independent Independent	6	7	9	7	10	8	8	12	11	13	13	15	15	14	13
Independent Republican	7	6	8	5	7	6	6	7	9	8	11	9	10	10	10
Weak Republican	14	14	14	17	14	16	14	15	15	15	13	14	14	13	14
Strong Republican	14	13	15	11	16	12	11	10	10	9	10	8	9	8	9
Apolitical	3	4	4	4	3	4	1	1	1	1	1	3	1	3	3
Total	100%	100%	100%	100%	100%	100%	100%	100%	100%	100%	100%	100%	100%	100%	100%
(N)	1784	1130	1757	1808	1911	1287	1550	1278	1553	1501	2694	2505	2850	2283	1407

Source: Center for Political Studies.

TABLE 5.2 ■ Defection Rates within Categories of Party Identification, 1952–1980

Party Identification	1952	1956	1960	1964	1968	1972	1976	1980
Democrat								
Strong	17[a]	15	9	5	11	26	9	14
Weak	39	37	28	18	38	52	25	40
Independent								
Democrat	40	33	15	11	49	44	24	55
Independent								
Republican	7	6	13	25	19	14	14	24
Republican								
Weak	6	7	13	43	12	9	22	14
Strong	1	1	2	10	3	4	3	18

Source: Center for Political Studies.
[a] Entry is the proportion of the voters whose vote for president was other than for the candidates of the parties with which they identified.

1980 election, 24 percent of the voting age population character-ized itself as some form of independent. Among other things, independents add a volatile and unpredictable element to the elec-torate. For example, over the last three decades, the independent vote has swung more than sixty percentage points in given elec-tions from one party to the other. In comparison, party identifiers provide a much more stable base for the vote (Table 5.2). For the years 1952–1980, the average defection rate among strong party identifiers was 18 percent, the fluctuation ranging between 5 and 26 percentage points, and for weak party identifiers, 25 percent with a range of 27 percentage points.

Even among those identifying with a political party, how-ever, there has been an erosion in the intensity of commitment (Table 5.1). The proportion of strong party identifiers is down by approximately one-third within the Democratic party and over 40 percent within the Republican party. While the number of weak party identifiers has remained stable in both parties, the number of "leaners" (those declaring themselves independent but appear-ing to favor one party or the other in their electoral behavior) is up 140 percent (and, of course, the proportion of "independent" independents has increased even more substantially).

Party attachments nevertheless remain a potent force in elec-tions. Roughly 50 percent of the electorate (down from three quarters of the voting age population in the fifties) still consider themselves members of one of the major political parties. Time is against the parties, however, and it may well be that party iden- 53 tification—a bond formed in childhood and thus one of great strength—may be the last indication of the true extent of the deterioration in party loyalty. Severe and persistent party defections and inconsistencies in electoral behavior may well precede any effort on the part of the individual to redefine his attitudinal attachments to the parties. The incidence of decreased party consistency in the vote in recent elections would indicate that this is the case. Norman H. Nie, Sidney Verba, and John P. Petrocik, in their revisionist examination of American voting behavior comment on the phenomena:

> . . . party affiliation was the central thread running through interpretations of American politics in the 1950s and 1960s. Citizen attitudes on issues appeared to be only slightly related one to another, and they were unstable enough over time to suggest that a high proportion of citizens had no meaningful issue positions. But party affiliation was a stable characteristic of the individual: it was likely to be inherited, it was likely to remain steady throughout the citizen's political life, and it was likely to grow in strength during that lifetime.

Even more important, party affiliation was related to other political phenomena. For the citizen, his sense of identification with a party was a guide to behavior; citizens voted for their party's candidates. It was a guide to understanding the political universe; candidates and issues were evaluated in party terms. Parties were objects of emotional attachment; citizens expressed positive feelings about their parties. Those citizens with partisan affiliation were the most active and involved citizens; partisanship appeared to be a force mobilizing citizens into political life. Partisanship gave continuity and direction to the political behavior of citizens and to American electoral life.[2]

The results of Nie, Verba, and Petrocik's analysis of "the changing American voter" led them to conclude that

1. Fewer citizens have a steady and strong psychological identification with a party.

2. Party affiliation is less of a guide to electoral choice.

3. Parties are less frequently used as standards of evaluation.

TABLE 5.3 ■ Age Differences in the Intensity of Party Support, 1980 Elections

Party Identification	Age Category			
	18–20 (%)		61 and Older (%)	
Democrats	30		49	
Strong		9		27
Weak		21		22
Independents	52		23	
Leaning Democratic		20		8
Pure Independents		20		9
Leaning Republican		12		7
Republicans	18		28	
Strong		4		14
Weak		14		4
Total	100%		100%	
(N)		66		306

Source: Center for Political Studies.

4. Parties are less frequently objects of positive feelings on the part of citizens. And

5. Partisanship is less likely to be transferred from generation to generation.[3]

Most alarmingly, these changes have taken place in just one generation.

There has been a decrease in the intensity of party identification among all subgroups within the population. Still, there are differences. The strongest and most consistent party identifiers are found in the oldest population groupings (those born in the first quarter of this century), and as these older voters die, the intensity of partisan identification for the population as a whole can be expected to further weaken.

The younger the age group, the weaker its attachments to political parties. For example, 52 percent of the young people entering the electorate in 1980 declared themselves independents, while 34 percent declared themselves Democrats and 14 percent Republicans. A comparison of 18-to-20 year olds with those over 50 makes the point vividly: The future favors independents.

Beyond the age factor—the most critical variable in the evolution of party ties—identifications in recent elections have remained stronger among residents of major urban areas, the poor, women, blacks, farmers, those with the least formal education, 55 and southerners (a remnant of the region's one-party heritage). The remnants of lingering New Deal coalitions can be seen in these distributions. Also, the income, educational, and professional levels of the increasingly independent electorate begin to suggest a bloc of voters capable of actively distinguishing between the parties and the candidates on a basis other than inherited party loyalties.

■■■■ THE RISE OF ISSUE VOTING

The major controversy in voting research today involves the role of "issue voting" in determining election outcomes. Is it less important, as important, or more important than party loyalty in determining election outcomes? The significance for the parties is clear. If issue voting is equal to or of greater importance in the vote decision than an individual's identification with a party, then both parties are going to have to do something they have long found difficult: stress issues in campaigns, develop coherent policy programs, take sharp and often antagonistic stands on the issues of greatest importance to the voting public in any given election, and educate the electorate to their positions and the reasons it should vote for them. Such a posture places enormous strains on an undisciplined, incoherent party system content with emphasizing the minimally effective bonds uniting its diverse coalitions. In any given election, the majority party prefers to trust the normal dynamics of party identifications to provide the margin of victory. The minority party, in turn, emphasizes short-term concerns detrimental to the majority party, hoping that these will produce the minimal defections from the majority party needed to win office. Neither party feels comfortable with issue-oriented campaigns, believing that the more specific it is in its policy commitments, the more likely it is to alienate a greater number of voters than it attracts. The more people who vote independent, the more obvious it is that change will come. The differences among analysts on issue voting, however, goes beyond this. Basically, scholars are divided into two camps: the "traditionalists," who continue to emphasize the importance, and even the primacy, of party loyalties in the vote decison and in determining election outcomes, and the "revisionists," who focus on the changes within the electorate and in the political environment that have increased the importance of issues in the voting calculus, often at the direct expense of party attachments.[4]

The revisionists make two points. First, the structure of the electorate has changed. It is younger, better-educated, and better-off financially, conditions that should allow for a more informed and more issue-oriented vote. Second, a change in the political temper of the times, brought about during the sixties in the controversies over Vietnam, along with continuing social disorders and abuse of government authority have made issues more significant in campaigns. The newer issues, whether they involve the environment or the limits of government power, generally fall outside the old coalitional boundaries and are not easily addressed within the New Deal coalitional limits (a division between the parties based on economic concerns). Consequently, party attachments continue to be important, but they may not be as important as first believed or as was claimed by studies of voting behavior based on analyses of electorates in the fifties. Issues have become increasingly more significant in influencing election outcomes and may now be the single most critical aspect in election decision-making.

The argument on both sides is complex and involves, among other things, an evolving conceptual and methodological reexamination of the ways in which data are gathered and analytic judgments are made. Nonetheless, a unity of views does appear to be emerging concerning the increasing importance of policy concerns in voting. By 1972, the Center for Political Studies of the University of Michigan—the foremost proponent of the traditionalist viewpoint, and the organization that has contributed the most to an understanding of modern electoral behavior—was willing to concede that the indicators they used to measure issue and ideological dimensions, "when taken together as reflecting ideology and policy voting, were substantially more important as direct explanations of the vote than was party identification."[5] Overall, *"as an explanation of the vote in 1972, issues were at least equally as important as party identification."*[6] (italics in original)

This represents a major concession by the traditionalists indications just how much the electorate and the forces working on voter decision-making have changed in a very short period of time. Party identification remains one of the more significant indicators in explaining national election outcomes, as the analyses of the 1976 and 1980 presidential votes have shown, but the rise of a more issue-oriented and potentially more ideological electorate has already begun to pressure political parties to perform in ways in which they have historically felt uncomfortable.

CHAPTER 6

PARTY LOYALTY AND RECENT ELECTIONS

■■

The presidential elections of 1976 and 1980 illustrate the destabilization of the national party system and the restructuring now taking place within the American electorate. As in all elections, the patterns of support for candidates and parties as well as the forces acting to influence the vote decision are open to differing political and scholarly interpretations. An understanding of the forces at work speaks to the complexities of a party system— and its influence on the vote—groping towards a redefinition of its role within electoral politics.

■■■ THE 1976 ELECTION

The 1976 presidential election heralded a return to party identification as the major and perhaps decisive factor influencing the vote. Or so it appeared to some analysts, who considered the events of the period 1960–1972 to be transitory and their harmful impacts limited. If so, then the party system could possibly return to the equilibrium it enjoyed during the New Deal/Fair Deal eras and the Eisenhower period.

To an extent, it was true: party identification was a more important influence on the vote in 1976 than it had been, for example, in 1972. Arthur E. Miller of the Center for Political Studies

TABLE 6.1 ▪ The Public's Assessment of the Nation's Business Climate, 1972–1980

Assessment[a]	1972 (%)	1974 (%)	1976 (%)	1978 (%)	1980 (%)
Better now than a year ago	40	37	47	35	13
Same as a year ago	30	23	17	18	15
Worse than a year ago	27	35	32	37	71
Don't know	3	5	4	10	1
Total	100%	100%	100%	100%	100%

Source: Center for Political Studies as Reported in Warren E. Miller, "Policy Directions and Presidential Leadership: Alternative Interpretations of the 1980 Presidential Election," unpublished paper delivered at the Annual Meeting of the American Political Science Association, New York, 1981.

[a] Pollster's question: Would you say at the present time business conditions are better or worse than they were a year ago?

concluded that "when the total effect of the major factors influencing the election are computed, our preliminary analyses show that party identification is the most important overall explanation of the electoral outcome."[1]

The assumption concerning the importance of party identification is correct. Party identification had a significantly higher correlation with the vote in 1976 than did issues or candidate evaluations (Table 6.1) and was more strongly correlated with the vote than in 1972, an election which witnessed a twenty-year low in the relationship between party identification and the vote and in which 42 percent of the Democratic party's identifiers defected to Richard Nixon. Unlike 1972, party identification was more significant than issues or candidate perceptions.

The results were not accidental. Jimmy Carter, the Democratic candidate, attempted to emphasize issues that would appeal to the badly divided Democratic coalition and that would place the Republican incumbent on the defensive. He largely succeeded in this strategy. Miller observed the following:

> In 1976 the Democratic candidate, Jimmy Carter,
> appeared to adopt a strategy of de-emphasizing those
> issues that had polarized the Democrats in 1972.
> Instead of articulating major policy differences
> between himself and Ford, Carter concentrated on
> issues that promised to reunite Democrats—issues
> such as unemployment, inflation, the Nixon pardon,

59

and the restoration of confidence in government. He avoided the so-called "social" issues that had divided the Democrats four years earlier. As the general election campaign proceeded, Carter placed increasing emphasis on the fact that he was a Democrat and on his desire to pull together the various factions within the party. The result of this campaign strategy was the re-emergence of party identification as a very strong determinant of vote choice.[2]

Carter's tactics were successful enough to win him the White House.

To a large degree, an attempt to read more into the 1976 outcome can be illusory. The trends of the previous decade or so were not reversed.

While the candidates of the two parties chose not to emphasize issue differences, little had changed among voters. Issue positions were not as strongly correlated with the vote in 1976 as in 1972, but "issue attitudes were equally as consistent at both time points" and policy preferences were clearly divergent (Table 6.2). Democrats held liberal positions on such issues as aid to minorities, the government's role in and responsibility for the economy, school busing to achieve integration, the rights accorded the accused in criminal proceedings, federally sponsored medical insurance, the equalization of tax policies, and penalties for marijuana use. The one point the party identifiers and the independents agreed upon was women's rights. Not surprisingly, Democrats consider themselves substantially more liberal than do Republicans. While policy differences between the parties may not relate as strongly to the vote in 1976 as they did in 1972, they continued to sharply divide the two partisan camps.

Ideological orientations in 1976 as in 1972 did show a strong relationship to the vote (79 percent of the liberals voted for Carter, 80 percent of the conservatives voted for Ford) and the association stands regardless of party identification.[3] The tenor of the campaign was intended to deemphasize ideological considerations. The fact that these considerations remained strongly correlated with the vote and that issue differences between the parties persisted, despite efforts to direct attention away from them, indicate that the changes observed in the electorate of the sixties and the early seventies were maintained.

This interpretation gains support from an analysis by Gerald M. Pomper. Pomper correlated the Democratic vote in the individual states in different elections in an attempt to establish the similarities in state coalitions for party candidates over time. His analysis emphasizes that the Carter vote in 1976 did not correlate with the vote given other Democratic candidates in recent elections (McGovern in 1972, Humphrey in 1968, and Johnson in 1964). It does show an association, however, with the New Deal years and the Stevenson–Kennedy vote. There is an association with the Truman (1948) and Humphrey (1968) coalitions only if the third party vote (for Strom Thurmond and George Wallace, respectively) is added. Even then, the correlations are not strong. What they do suggest is that the Carter–Ford vote was significantly different from that of other recent elections and that the coalitional nature of the traditional support patterns for the two parties changed during the sixties. Carter, through sheer will and an effective campaign strategy, was able to return if only temporarily to the general coalitional base of an earlier era.

Even then this achievement may not be as impressive as it once seemed. Running against a flawed incumbent—a man who granted Richard Nixon a full pardon (which was a significant factor in the vote), a man who had never conducted a national campaign, who had barely won his party's renomination, and whose administration had been saddled with both high inflation and high unemployment rates (its "misery index," as his opponent labeled it)—Carter was only able to squeeze out a narrow victory (51 percent of the popular two-party vote to Ford's 49 percent). This, at a time when the Democrats held a decisive edge in party identification (51 percent to the Republicans' 33 percent), meant then there were considerable defections among partisans (29 percent of the weak Democrats and 9 percent of the strong Democrats and 22 percent of the weak Republicans and 3 percent of the strong Republicans identifiers voted for the opposition party's candidate), tendencies more indicative of those characterizing recent elections than those associated with an earlier "stable-party period."

There is further evidence that, despite the explanation advanced for the outcome, the position of the parties within the electorate continued to deteriorate. Arthur Miller has commented that

> . . . the reappearance of a strong direct effect of party
> identification on vote choice in 1976 does not
> necessarily imply that the trend toward weakening
> party loyalty, evident in the United States since the

TABLE 6.2 ■ Differences among Supporters of the Presidential Candidates by Policy Preferences, 1980

	Carter Democrats	Reagan Democrats	Other Reagan Voters	Anderson Voters	Total Carter Voters	Total Reagan Voters
Policy Preferences						
Defense spending						
Decrease	17.6	5.4	4.3	19.7	17.0	4.6
Stay the same	19.4	15.3	13.2	22.4	20.1	13.7
Increase	63.0	79.3	82.5	57.9	63.0	81.8
Government spending						
Reduce	13.3	39.8	59.9	35.1	15.3	54.6
In-between	18.6	16.7	20.1	18.9	19.6	19.6
No reduction	68.1	43.5	20.1	45.9	65.0	25.8
Tax cut						
None	33.7	17.1	16.9	31.3	32.6	16.9
10%	24.1	15.8	17.2	26.6	24.2	16.9
20%	18.1	31.6	20.6	15.6	18.5	23.0
30% or more	24.1	35.5	45.3	26.6	24.6	43.1
ERA						
Approve	76.0	52.7	40.5	76.6	75.5	43.5
Disapprove	24.0	47.3	59.5	23.4	24.5	56.6

Carter Approval						
Iran						
Approve	65.9	20.9	15.1	21.1	65.6	16.4
Disapprove	34.1	79.1	84.9	78.9	34.4	83.6
Inflation						
Approve	47.7	12.6	4.6	11.5	47.9	6.6
Disapprove	52.3	87.4	95.4	88.5	52.1	93.4
Performance Assessments						
Solve economic problems						
Carter better	55.3	8.6	2.4	17.1	46.0	3.4
Same	35.7	23.8	13.6	44.7	45.2	24.7
Reagan better	8.9	67.6	84.0	38.2	8.9	71.9
Provide strong leadership						
Carter better	55.9	8.8	2.3	17.5	46.2	3.6
Same	33.6	15.9	8.2	28.8	43.6	15.2
Reagan better	10.5	75.2	89.5	53.8	10.2	81.2
Develop good foreign relations						
Carter better	75.9	27.4	12.9	39.0	60.8	14.8
Same	17.3	−27.4	24.4	39.0	33.7	32.4
Reagan better	7.8	45.3	62.6	22.1	5.5	52.8

Source: Center for Political Studies as reported in Arthur H. Miller and Martin Wattenberg, "Policy and Performance in the 1980 Election," a paper presented at the Annual Meeting of the American Political Science Association, 1981.

mid-sixties, has been attested. On the contrary, evidence suggests that attitudes toward the parties have maintained their negative direction and that attachment to the party system, when viewed more generally than presidential vote choice alone, has continued to weaken.

Respect for the parties as institutions of representation . . . decreased during that time: The proportion of the eligible electorate believing that political parties help a "good deal" in making the government pay attention to what the people think dropped from roughly 40 per cent in 1964 to 29 percent in 1972, and to only 18 percent in 1976.

Furthermore, continued deterioration in the public's ties to the party system was also revealed by behavioral indicators. Defection from party loyalty at the congressional level (House of Representatives)—as revealed by the proportion of individuals casting a vote for the party other than the one they identify with—remained quite high in 1976.

While none of these defection rates reflect historical highs for the elections of the past quarter-century, they also do not fall significantly below the high defection rates of the last decade. The incidence of split-ticket voting (between presidential and congressional levels) showed a similar decline from the high point attained in 1972, but still remained noticeably above that found during the 'fifties. Republicans, in fact, registered a new record for ticket-splitting (24 percent).

Thus, the voters in 1976 were effectively expressing disenchantment with the party system at the same time that many of them were voting for their party's presidential nominee.[4]

A final note on 1976. Evaluations of economic conditions (inflation and unemployment), the administration's job ratings in these regards, and the voter's expectations concerning which party or candidate was likely to better handle these problems did affect the election outcome. These were issues that Carter stressed to his advantage. The tactic would come back to haunt him four years later.

▬▬ THE 1980 ELECTION

Jimmy Carter had little going for him at the beginning of the 1980 campaign and he knew it. His own staff believed he was "a president deeply in trouble." As his pollster Patrick Caddell later said: "There was no way we could survive either a primary or a general election contest if we allowed it to become a referendum on the first three years of the Carter administration."[5]

Carter's major strength appeared to be his identification with the majority Democratic party, a point he had emphasized repeatedly in 1976 to good effect. By 1980, however, his ties to the mainstream of the Democratic party's coalition were badly strained. In particular, the liberal wing of the Democratic party found little to support in the Carter candidacy. As one prominent liberal spokesman said, "I cannot see that on his record President Carter has earned twenty more seconds—not to speak of four more years—in the White House."[6] The unions, a core element of the Democratic coalition, were bitter toward the White House. "Carter ignored the steel workers for three and a half years, and now he comes asking for our votes. Well, he's not getting them," said one union official.[7] Douglas Fraser, president of the UAW (United Automobile Workers), one of the largest and most active of the unions, explained to an interviewer: "We've always told our people to vote their pocketbooks, and this year they may do it."[8] Ironically, a laborer voting his pocketbook in 1980 meant an anti-Democratic vote.

The Demographic and Political Implications of the Group Vote

The vote breakdown demonstrated the President's inability to hold his coalition together. Carter lost many of his previous supporters while Reagan, however, was able to keep two-thirds of the Ford voters. The coalition that supported Carter in 1976 showed sizeable defections in 1980 (see Table 3.3 in Chapter 3). Particularly pronounced, as previously noted, was the decrease in support among males, whites, manual and white collar workers, older voters, voters with only a high school education, Catholics, labor union families, and residents of the West and the South. The defection of both strong and weak Democratic party identifiers in 1980 was the most salient in the history of contemporary polling, the one exception being the ill-fated McGovern candidacy in 1972.

Among Democratic party identifiers and independents, Carter lost votes from liberals and moderates, but actually gained   65 some support from liberal and moderate Republicans who found Reagan's staunch conservatism unappealing. Ideologically, and without reference to party identification, Carter's support among liberals fell 13 percentage points and among moderates, 9 percentage points. The only group to support Carter strongly in both 1976 and 1980 were blacks. Overall, it was not an impressive performance.[9]

Issues and Candidate Perceptions

Ronald Reagan asked viewers in the last presidential debate, televised the week before the election, if they were better off now than they had been before. If so, the implication was that they should vote for Jimmy Carter. If not, it was time for a change and Ronald Reagan was the man to bring it about. It was an ingenious appeal, focusing attention on the floundering economy and the negative evaluations of Carter's stewardship in office. Coupled with a conscious effort to defuse the right-wing extremism and irresponsibility the Carter people attempted to associate with the Reagan campaign, the appeal proved strong enough to impress undecided voters (depending on the poll, 25 percent to 37 percent of the electorate, the highest in three decades)[10] with the impracticality of continuing with Carter and the reasonableness of trusting the government to Reagan. Apparently, the last debate was enough to turn the tide in Reagan's favor and begin a movement that within days gave the Republicans a substantial edge in the final vote.[11]

An analysis of the survey data from the 1980 election provides an indication of what the public was thinking. When asked if business conditions were better than a year ago, seven out of ten voters said they were worse, a jump of over 30 percentage points in two years, and by far the most depressing assessment of the decade (Table 6.2). Analyzing the differences in issue positions among the groups supporting the various candidates reveals substantial divergences: Voters did perceive emphatic differences between the candidates on policy questions, which influenced their decision, while the resulting coalitions showed sharp and contradictory policy preferences (Table 6.2). For example, those who favored a major tax cut, a reduction in government spending, and a larger military budget voted for Reagan. Those who approved of the ERA and Carter's handling of the Iranian hostage situation and who believed Carter stronger than Reagan on foreign policy issues

TABLE 6.3 ■ Assessment of Carter's Economic Record and Job Performance

Month	Presidential Approval[a]	Inflation	Unemployment
February	+18	−30	+1
April	−12	−48	−20
June	−23	−49	−42
October	−18	−49	−33

Source: Center for Political Studies as Reported in Warren E. Miller, "Policy Directions and Presidential Leadership: Alternative Interpretations of the 1980 Presidential Election," unpublished paper delivered at the Annual Meeting of the American Political Science Association, New York, 1981.
[a] Entries are the proportion approving Carter's performance minus the proportion disapproving, in response to pollster's question: Do you approve or disapprove of the way Jimmy Carter is handling (his job as President/inflation/unemployment)?

generally backed the President. Overwhelmingly, the Reagan voters (including those defecting from the Democratic party) rejected Carter's handling of the economy, and more specifically the administration's policies on inflation, and they looked to Reagan to provide strong leadership and to resolve the nation's economic plight. To the extent that Reagan can claim a mandate, this would seem to be it.

Among those who felt their own economic positions had improved, Carter did well (see Table 6.9). If their economic position had worsened, their support of the President fell proportionately. This was as true of Democrats, liberals, and union households—normally bulwarks of the Democratic party's vote—as it was of Republicans. "Economic dissatisfaction," says Gerald M. Pomper, "is the most direct influence on the 1980 vote, and it had greater impact than any other issue."[12] The conclusion seems justified.

Carter's inability to manage the economic crisis negatively affected his job ratings (Table 6.3). The negative evaluations of Carter's handling of his office and, more specifically, inflation and unemployment, increased over the course of the election year.[13] William Schneider has plotted Carter's ratings on a variety of issues for the turbulent year leading up to the election. One is impressed by how consistently, and depressingly, low they were in each of the areas examined: the economy; foreign affairs; overall job performance; and the handling of the Iranian hostage situation. On these points, all the polls agreed. Schneider remarked that Carter "entered the 1980 campaign with the lowest job approval ratings 67 of any incumbent since the Gallup began taking these measurements in the 1940s." Given these "terrible" ratings, "It is remarkable that the election was considered too close to call right up until the last minute."[14]

Reagan's Appeal

Ronald Reagan's greatest assets may have been that he was running against Jimmy Carter, that times were bad, and that voters were looking for an alternative. None of these factors, of course, hurt his campaign. Neither Carter nor Reagan was a particularly strong or well-liked candidate, the public's image of both men ranking among the all-time lows.[15] Nonetheless, Reagan did have a number of strengths as a campaigner, all of which he put to good use. He is a fine politician with good instincts, qualities that are often underestimated by opponents. Since his early campaigns in the sixties for governor of California, during his tenure as governor, and during his various campaigns for the Republican presidential nomination (beginning in 1968), opponents have tended to dismiss him as an actor with little substance or appeal. This worked in Reagan's favor. He has a likeable, even charming, personality that projects well over television—as a consequence, often undercutting many of the charges made against him—and he is a good speaker with the ability to simplify and personalize complex issues. An experienced performer, he was able to transmit a sense of substance, trustworthiness, and command to television audiences that served him well in the 1980 campaign. These qualities were evident from the New Hampshire primary to election day. A comparison of Reagan's presentation and delivery in the last televised debate with President Carter provided a contrast that worked in Reagan's favor.

The images Carter and Reagan projected were reflectd by the polls (Table 6.4), Gallup reporting that Reagan was viewed as a strong, decisive leader with a well-defined program while Carter was seen as religious and moral. Given the times and economic conditions, Reagan had enough appeal to offer a viable alternative to the incumbent and his policies.

Congressional Elections

The results of the congressional races were more surprising than the presidential outcome. For the first time in a generation, the Republicans could claim control of one of the houses of the Con-

TABLE 6.4 ■ The Public's Perceptions of Carter and Reagan in 1980

Question: "Here is a list of terms—shown as pairs of opposites—that have been used to describe (Jimmy Carter/Ronald Reagan). From each pair of opposites, would you select the term which you feel best describes (Carter/Reagan)?"

	Carter (%)[a]	Reagan (%)
Carter Rated Higher		
A religious person	87	40
Takes moderate, middle-of-the-road positions	82	48
Sympathetic to problems of the poor	68	41
A man of high moral principles	83	70
Sides with the average citizen	56	43
Says what he believes even if unpopular	57	54
Reagan Rated Higher		
Has strong leadership abilities	31	65
Decisive, sure of himself	37	69
Has a well-defined program for moving the country ahead	27	53
You know where he stands on issues	33	54
A colorful, interesting personality	50	70
The kind of person who can get the job done	39	56
Offers imaginative, innovative solutions to national problems	37	52
Has modern, up-to-date solutions to national problems	39	51
Has well thought out, carefully considered solutions for national problems	36	45
Has a clear understanding of the issues facing the country	50	55
No Difference		
Bright, intelligent	73	73
Would display good judgment in a crisis	55	55

Source: Gallup polls as reported in William Schneider, "The November 4 Vote for President: What Did it Mean?" Austin Ranney, ed., *The American Elections of 1980*, Washington, D.C.: American Enterprise Institute, 1981.
[a] Figures exclude respondents who did not express an opinion.

gress. They won 12 Senate seats (and control of the Senate, 53 to 47) and 33 House seats from the Democrats (who still managed to control the House, but by a diminished margin, 243–192). This shift in power, along with the margin of victory in the presidential race (10 percentage points), was enough for Reagan to claim a mandate for a new direction in public policy. Through skillful political direction, the president was able to marshall public opinion, his own troops, and enough defections from the conservative wing of a dispirited Democratic party to win a series of stunning legislative victories. Included among these triumphs was a "supply side" budget, a 25 to 30 percent cut in federal taxes, a severe reduction of domestic programs, a major increase in military appropriations, and, under the banner of a "new federalism," an attempt to shift responsibility for many program areas—from education, transportation, and environmental protection to welfare—to the state. The legislative achievements were extraordinary, even if the results of the new policies weren't—the economy was still floundering, unemployment was on the increase, inflation rates remained high, and the goal of a balanced budget was abandoned when faced with future deficits of historic proportions. Reagan's first year in office was compared to Lyndon Johnson's and Franklin Roosevelt's.

The Democrats came out of the 1980 election disorganized and badly beaten. Not only had they lost control of the Senate, but many of their best-known and most prestigious congressional leaders had been defeated, often by young, relatively unknown candidates, many of whom had taken advantage of the communication, media, and financial resources made available by the newly powerful PACs. After the election, many of the ideological PACs of the "New Right," the Moral Majority, and the antiabortion movement would claim the election represented a display of their political muscle and a vindication of their programs. For them, the election constituted a demand for drastic changes in social policies.

The claims are debatable. It is unlikely that the single-issue and ideological PACs exercised the influence on the election that they believed. Furthermore, the public's views on social policies are far more complex and less supportive of their policies than PACs claimed. For example, there is no evidence of a major swing (or any movement, for that matter, between elections) in a conservative direction on significant policy dimensions (Table 6.5). The number of liberals has fluctuated between 16 and 21 percent in the last three presidential elections and the number of conservatives between 25 and 28 percent. What has increased is the proportion of voters who cannot or will not identify themselves ideologically. In the same period (1972–1980), opposition to civil rights gains decreased; views on abortion remained stable (and mostly proabortion); support for the women's movement increased (and it too is strongly pro-women's rights); the opposition to busing declined in intensity, but 73 percent of the electorate

TABLE 6.5 ■ Self-identification of Liberalism/Conservativism among the Public, 1972–1980

Ideology	1972	1974	1976	1978	1980
Liberal	19	21	16	20	16
Center	27	26	25	27	19
Conservative	27	26	25	28	27
Not placed	28	27	33	27	38
Total	100%	100%	100%	100%	100%

Source: Center for Political Studies as Reported in Warren E. Miller, "Policy Directions and Presidential Leadership: Alternative Interpretations of the 1980 Presidential Election," unpublished paper delivered at the Annual Meeting of the American Political Science Association, New York, 1981.

still opposed it in 1980; those favoring government aid to blacks and other minorities decreased somewhat; support for greater spending on behalf of defense remained firm; and the proportion of people believing that the government should see to it that everyone had a job and a decent standard of living stayed about the same.[16]

The most decided change occurred in the number of people who believed that the government in Washington was too powerful for the good of the country or the individual (Table 6.6), a trend that since 1964 has become more pervasive. It is a feeling that Jimmy Carter, an "outsider," capitalized on in the race against Gerald Ford in 1976 and, ironically, one that Ronald Reagan used to advantage against incumbent Carter in 1980. When 1980 is compared with 1976, little change is evident in the totals. If there is a mandate there, it is one of long duration.

TABLE 6.6 ■ Public Perception of the Power of the Federal Government, 1964–1980

Perception[a]	1964[b]	1966	1968	1970	1972	1976	1978	1980
Too powerful	30	39	41	31	41	49	43	48
Not too powerful	36	27	30	33	27	20	14	15
Don't know, no opinion	34	34	29	36	32	31	43	37
Total	100%	100%	100%	100%	100%	100%	100%	100%

Source: Gallup polls as reported in William Schneider, "The November 4 Vote for President: What Did it Mean?" Austin Ranney, ed., The American Elections of 1980, Washington, D.C.: American Enterprise Institute, 1981.
[a] Pollster's question: Some people are afraid the government in Washington is getting too powerful for the good of the country and the individual. Others feel that the government in Washington is not getting too strong. Do you have an opinion on this or not?
[b] In percent.

TABLE 6.7 ■ Spending Priorities of Citizens for Government Programs, 1980

Too Little	Too Much	About Right
Defense/Military (60%)[a]	Foreign aid (73%)	Blacks (40%)
Crime (59%)	Welfare (55%)	Environment (38%)[b]
Drug addiction (52%)	Space (41%)	
Education (50%)		
Health (47%)		
Environment (38%)		

Source: Center for Political Studies as Reported in Warren E. Miller, "Policy Directions and Presidential Leadership: Alternative Interpretations of the 1980 Presidential Election," unpublished paper delivered at the Annual Meeting of the American Political Science Association, New York, 1981.

[a] Figures in parentheses represent the proportion of those polled supporting the position.

[b] Thirty-eight percent of the respondents thought "too little" was being spent on environment protection and another 38 percent thought that the spending level was "about right."

Also, most voters believed too little was being spent on everything from education and health to military hardware and crime prevention (Table 6.7). They were satisfied with the levels of expenditure on blacks and their problems and on the environment, but felt too much was spent on foreign aid, welfare, and the space program. Possibly there was a mandate for change in these figures—economic conditions demanded some resolution—but whether the changes were as all-encompassing or in the direction the new president, the Congress, or the interest groups most active in the election believed is open to question.

The Aftermath

Nonetheless, the Democrats and the "liberals" found themselves at a distinct disadvantage. In the Senate, many prominent party leaders were defeated—Frank Church (Id.), George McGovern (S.D.), Birch Bayh (Ind.), Gaylord Nelson (Wis.), Warren Magnuson (Wash.), Herman Talmadge (Ga.), and John Culver (Io.). They were replaced by younger, more conservative senators whose views will make a mark on national politics. Charles E. Jacob commented that

> . . . we are looking at a Republican sweep that is also a conservative sweep. Every freshman Republican (except for two who rejected PAC support) was endorsed by one or more conservative groups in 1980. Moreover, those sponsored Republicans elected

to the Senate from seats in the House, and who
therefore brought with them conservative records,
had 1979 ACA scores [Americans for Constitutional
Action, a conservative group] as follows: Symms, 100
percent; Quale, 91 percent; Grassley, 88 percent;
Abdnor, 96 percent; and Andrews, 88 percent. On
the other hand, the Democratic incumbent losers,
except for the four Deep Southerners, were liberal
stalwarts for many years. Indeed, in the face of the
concerted NCPAC [National Conservative Political
Action Committee] assault begun against several of
them a year before the election, some Senate liberal
leaders moderated their positions through 1979, thus
appearing less fully liberal than normally.
Congressional Quarterly reported in 1980 that . . .
liberal Democratic senators (some of whom would be
reelected in the fall) received ADA scores [Americans
for Democratic Action, a liberal group] on average
ten points below the previous year's tally. In sum,
political behavior in the Senate of the 97th Congress
should be markedly more conservative than it has
been in many years, due to the sweep of conservative
Republicans. One detects no Javitses, Mathiases, or
Weickers in this freshman contingent.[17]

Jacob's prophesy has proven true for the Congress as a whole.

The 1980 election may prove to be an example of "retrospective" or "performance-based" voting.[18] As Arthur H. Miller
and Martin P. Wattenberg, in their review of the election, put it:
"The voters did not reject Jimmy Carter simply for lack of a winning personality. They acted out of their perceived best interest
and in the best interest of the country by voting on the basis of
their assessments of the candidates' capabilities to provide prosperity at home and prestige abroad."[19] They had had four years
under Carter in which to evaluate his competence as president.

Party indentification was again important in 1980, but it
worked against Reagan's candidacy. Evaluations of Carter's performance and of the impact of governmental policies generally,
preferences for policy changes, issue positions, and ideological
predispositions were all significant contributors to the vote. Overall, a desire for a change in policy direction, evaluations of the
performance of the Carter administration, and ideological pref- 73

erence, in order, worked to elect Reagan. Against him, in order, were the party-identified vote, views on issues, and candidate-related effects.[20] If this is confusing and less clear-cut than one might desire, the words of Warren Miller might offer some solace: "It should be remembered that the general issue of spending on domestic services . . . demonstrates that popular support for a liberal policy *and* for a conservative change in the direction of governmental action concerning that policy can co-exist."[21] They can and do co-exist. Policy preferences are overlaid by practical evaluations of the incumbent and his execution of the office, the severity of the challenges confronting him, and the necessity of confining the choice realistically to the two major-party candidates.

■■■■ THE CONGRESSIONAL ELECTIONS OF 1982

If the conservatives and possibly even the far right received a mandate from the 1980 elections, it was short-lived. In 1982 the Republicans lost twenty-six seats in the House, considerably fewer than the forty some seats that had been predicted but well above the fifteen Jimmy Carter's party lost in the midterm elections of 1978. The Republicans maintained their edge in the Senate, but the replacement of members in both parties favored moderate and centrist rather than extremist positions, a development that caused the Reagan administration increasing problems in dealing with the Congress.

Basically there are three models used to explain off-year congressional elections. First, there is the "surge and decline" model put forward by Angus Campbell.[22] This approach emphasizes the short-term dynamics associated with presidential elections—the campaign hoopla, media emphasis, issue concerns, candidate perceptions, and the political and economic environment in which the election takes place, all of which serve to increase voter interest and voter turnout. The result is that many "peripheral" voters, who do not participate in off-year congressional elections, are attracted to presidential elections. As a consequence, it is argued that the off-year electorate is not only considerably smaller, but that it is a more committed electorate, more partisan and more typical of the real voting constituency in the country. Partisanship is expected to play a bigger role in determining off-year outcomes.

The second model emphasizes the referendum aspects of off-year elections.[23] In these analyses, off-year elections can be interpreted as a response to and judgment on the president's program. Grievances against the administration in power come into play and the outcome of the election sets the tone for the administration's remaining two years in office.

Finally, there is the model that emphasizes the advantages of the incumbent in seeking reelection and the isolation, uniqueness, and local service character of congressional district races.[24] Seen from this perspective, these races are personal judgments by individual congressional electorates on their representatives. In any such contest, the incumbent would have the position, the backlog of goodwill, constituency service record, and funding to ensure enormous advantages in the race for reelection.

All three explanatory approaches can contribute to an understanding of the 1982 congressional results. Certainly, the off-year electorate was considerably smaller than that of presidental years. The return of many Democrats who defected to Reagan in 1980—union workers, blue collar workers, the economically disadvantaged—helps explain the Democratic gains. The ability of the Republican National Committee and the Republican congressional and Senate campaign committees to adequately fund congressional races, supply their candidates with technological and professional expertise, and run national media and polling campaigns—efforts not matched by their Democratic counterparts—was generally believed to have averted disastrous midterm losses of from twelve to eighteen additional seats.[25]

The results of the off-year election were believed to represent a negative reaction to the Reagan administration's policies. There is evidence to back this referendum-type assessment. Eighty percent of the voters felt the economy was the chief issue in the campaign; 49 percent believed the condition of the economy was worse than it had been a year before, as opposed to 25 percent who thought it was better; 58 percent were dissatisfied with the condition the country was in.[26] Curiously, while the electorate disapproved of the administration's policies, the President himself remained relatively popular. The number of those disapproving of Reagan's job performance had increased 10 percentage points, from 31 to 41 percent between June of 1981 and election day 1982, yet one-half of the population (52 percent) still approved of the President's performance in office.[27]

TABLE 6.8 ■ Reasons Given for Congressional Vote, 1982

	Voted	
Reason for Vote	Republican	Democrat
Preference for candidate	26[a]	25
Pro-/anti-party	17	21
Economic policy	16	16
Spending: too much/too little by government	12	3
Pro-/anti-Reagan	9	5
Group mentions		15
Social Security		2

Source: John R. Petrocik and Fred T. Steeper, "Economic Issues and the Local Candidate in the 1982 Congressional Election," a paper prepared for delivery at the Annual Meeting of the Midwest Association for Public Opinion Research, November 19–20, Chicago, Illinois, 1982.
[a] Table entry is percent giving the indicated reason.

As for the local service-incumbency model, John R. Petrocik and Fred T. Steeper have estimated an average difference of +11 percentage points between the base party vote in a district and the support given an incumbent.[28] In the same study, one out of four voters gave candidate appeal as the reason for their vote, followed by party loyalty, economic policy considerations, and support for or opposition to Reagan (Table 6.8). For the 1982 election year as a whole, Petrocik and Steeper plotted the relevance of different issues and perceptions in influencing the vote decision and how these changed over the course of the campaign (Table 6.9). Party identification correlated highly with the vote, as did a perception of who was responsible for the recession (the Republican national media campaign blamed previous Democratic administrations and Democratic Congresses). Other issues relevant to the election outcome included: an evaluation of the effectiveness of the Reagan programs; Reagan's job approval rating; overall economic satisfaction; a belief in the fairness of the administration's approach (the Democrats emphasized that the Reagan programs favored the rich and discriminated against the poor and minorities); and the judgment of economic progress compared to a year ago.

Overall, the verdict was mixed. President Reagan and the Republicans lost a substantial number of seats in the Congress, although not the number they might have. While Reagan remained popular with a majority of voters, his policies did not. If the trends apparent in 1982 continue, and if economic conditions fail to improve, the Reagan administration can expect increasing resistance

TABLE 6.9 ■ Factors Affecting the 1982 Congressional Vote Campaign Period: Correlation between Vote Intention and Perceptions of the Economy, Reagan, and His Programs: Various Dates

	February 1982		May 1982		July 1982		September 1982		October 1982		November 1982	
	Zero Order	Partial	Zero Order	Partial	Zero Order	Partial	Zero Order	Partial	Zero Order	Partial	Zero Order	Partial
Party Identification	.78		.76		.77		.75		.71		.67	
Reagan Job Approval	.61	.30	.59	.31	.58	.27	.49	.23	.56	.29	.54	.27
Current Economy												
Overall satisfaction—general	.48	.25	.42	.21	.45	.23	.35	.16	.43	.19	.43	.23
Satisfaction/dissatisfaction with unemployment	.24	.12	.21	.07	.21	.08	.23	.08	NA	NA	.23	.14
Satisfaction/dissatisfaction with inflation	.18	NS	.10	NS	.07	NS	.12	NS	NA	NA	.08	NS
Perception of current economy	.30	.12	.27	.12	.33	.12	.27	.09	.40	.22	.37	.20
Expectations for economy	.39	.17	.39	.21	.33	.14	.28	.15	.32	.14	.21	.09
Personal Economic Condition	.22	.08	.22	.07	.27	.10	.23	.12	NA	NA	.30	.13
Responsibility for Recession	.50	NS	.43	.18	.50	.22	.49	.23	.49	.22	.54	.31
Reagan Program												
Effectiveness	.38	.18	.42	.21	.36	.15	.39	.17	NA	NA	.49	.29
Fairness to all Americans	.55	.23	.53	.26	.53	.29	.48	.23	.45	.23	.47	.22

Source: John R. Petrocik and Fred T. Steeper, "Economic Issues and the Local Candidate in the 1982 Congressional Election," a paper prepared for delivery at the Annual Meeting of the Midwest Association for Public Opinion Research, November 19–20, Chicago, Illinois, 1982.

from the Congress to its initiatives and a spirited challenge for the White House from the Democrats in 1984.

■■■ CONCLUSION

An analysis of the returns from the 1976, 1980, and 1982 elections reinforces the picture of a confused, frustrated electorate seeking answers to problems that a succession of candidates and party positions have so far been unable to satisfactorily provide. It is an electorate in transition, which adds a dimension of complexity to analyses and an unpredictability to election outcomes that was evident in each election year. These conditions continued into the early prenomination voting in the 1984 election year.

CHAPTER 7

Parties at the National Level

Organizationally, American political parties are truly unique. Reputedly, they—

- are undisciplined, noncohesive aggregations of local, district, and national party entities with considerable jurisdictional and operational overlapping.

- enjoy no authority structure of consequence, enforcing few demands and with limited or no sanctions to discipline, reward, or promote members.

- have no clear lines of communication, no centralized decision-making, and, in organizational terms, no clear purpose beyond the vague mandate "to win elections."

- have no defined membership qualifications, a rarity for bureaucratic organizations. The line between group (party) and nongroup (nonparty) member is blurred at best and highly permeable. In fact, there is no universal definition of what constitutes party membership, most settling for the psychological association contained within an individual's head (i.e., those who consider themselves members are, those who do not consider themselves members are not).

- have no set expectations of the obligations membership makes on the individual, whether he is a voter, party official, or public officeholder.

79

■   are more controlled by and responsive to local party and po-
    litical needs than they are to more centralized party direction
    (state or national). Put another way, power is lodged in the
    local party units closest to the voter. The higher one ascends
    in the party hierarchy, the less control and influence one has
    within the party apparatus.

This is not the type of picture that emerges when one thinks
of the Defense Department, the AMA (American Medical Association), the UAW (United Auto Workers), the Menninger
Clinic, U.S. Steel or any other bureaucratic organization one can
conjure up. Yet it is the description of party organization in the
United States that has been passed on to generations of students.

■■■■ AMERICAN PARTIES IN INTERNATIONAL PERSPECTIVE

Kenneth Janda, who has done the most extensive analyses of party
structures in a cross-national, comparative framework, has established the distinctive nature of American parties when viewed in
a world context. Janda examined 153 political parties from all parts
of the world that operated during the period 1950–1962. He scored
them on twelve dimensions, eight relating to external and environmental pressures affecting party structures and four relating to
"internal organization."[1] It is these last four that we are concerned
with.

The four dimensions used comparatively to assess the organizational attributes of political parties included:

1.   Degree of organization, or structural complexity, of the par-
    ties. This factor does not refer to power distributions, but to
    the *complexity* of the parties' structural properties. It measures
    the extent to which party structures are formally articulated
    and specified in law, party by-laws, or by tradition.

2.   Centralization of power. This dimension corresponds to
    what is commonly associated with bureaucratic structure, the
    locus of power within the organization. In almost all organ-
    izations, power is highly centralized.

3.   Organizational coherence, a measure of cohesion and fac-
    tionalism within party organizations.

4.   Organizational involvement, the extent of the behavioral and
    motivational commitment to the party.[2]

While all four dimensions are important, the first two—structural differentiation of parties and power distributions within the organizations—are particularly relevant to this inquiry.

Janda's first finding is not surprising and supports what many believed: the two American parties are extremely close to each other on the four dimensions analyzed. This consequently allows for a composite measure, or average of the two sets of scores, to be used for comparative purposes in the tables below without doing harm to the relative placement of either party. The second finding dramatically confirms popular assumptions: the two American parties, still scored separately, rank at the very bottom of most of the indices of organization, involvement, power, coherence, and policy cohesiveness. In fact, the American parties rank with other groups that are considered at best borderline examples of political parties, in the literal sense of the term.

Table 7.1 contrasts the composite indicators of the American parties with the group scores for competitive party systems in Western Europe, other non-European competitive party systems, and noncompetitive parties in general. As the table shows, political parties in the United States rank last by a wide margin on the measures of centralization of power, organizational coherence, and organizational involvement. They score considerably better on structural differentiation (degree of organization), about equaling the European parties. What this means is that the Democratic and Republican parties, at least on paper, have highly complex and well-regulated party bureaucracies and that party units of one sort or another can be found in most localities and at most levels. It is also a reflection of the extensive statutory regulation of party agencies and the various party by-laws that define jurisdictions, funding practices, activities on behalf of candidates, and organizational participation in elections. What this measure does not indicate is the power and control the party hierarchies exercise, the extent of the activities, and the commitment to and definition of the party as a group independent of others and influential on the political scene. By such measures, the American parties rank low and are in fact among the most organizationally inarticulate, incohesive, and loosely integrated parties to be found anywhere.

NATIONAL PARTY ORGANIZATION

The essence of the national parties—whom they represent and whom they serve—was captured in a byplay that involved the 81

TABLE 7.1 ▪ American Political Parties in International Perspective

Party Grouping	Mean Value	Standard Deviation	(N)
Comparison of Parties on Degree of Organization			
United States	.075	.09	(2)
Western European competitive	.08	.84	(42)
Non-European competitive	−.37	.80	(54)
Noncompetitive	−.08	.80	(46)
All parties outside United States	−.14	.82	(142)[a]
Comparison of Parties on Centralization of Power			
United States	1.39	.03	(2)
Western European competitive	−.08	.49	(42)
Non-European competitive	−.09	.81	(56)
Noncompetitive	.37	.62	(47)
All parties outside United States	.06	.70	(145)
Comparison of Parties on Coherence			
United States	−.76	.05	(2)
Western European competitive	.07	.66	(42)
Non-European competitive	−.07	.83	(55)
Noncompetitive	−.06	.69	(43)
All parties outside United States	−.02	.74	(140)[b]
Comparison of Parties on Involvement			
United States	−.77	.00	(2)
Western European competitive	.07	.60	(42)
Non-European competitive	−.16	.74	(55)
Noncompetitive	−.03	.88	(45)
All parties outside United States	−.05	.75	(142)[c]

Source: Kenneth Janda, "A Comparative Analysis of Party Organizations: The United States, Europe, and the World," in William Crotty, ed., *The Party Symbol*, San Francisco: W. H. Freeman, 1980.
[a] Three parties could not be scored on degree of organization.
[b] Five parties could not be scored on coherence.
[c] Three parties could not be scored on involvement.

Republican National Committee and the Reagan White House. The incident occurred near the end of Ronald Reagan's first year as president and excited little interest. It was business as usual for the national parties.

The flap involved the Republican National Chairman, Richard Richards, a conservative appointed by Reagan right after his election (actually, the Republican and Democratic chairs are elected by their respective national committees, but with a sitting president this is but a formality). Richards had speculated in an interview in November of 1981 that two administration officials under fire, David Stockman, Director of the Bureau of the Budget, and Richard V. Allen, national security advisor, would be leaving the administration and that Reagan might not seek a second term.[3] The White House was infuriated by what it believed to be Richards' indiscretion. Consequently, Reagan immediately appointed a deputy chairman who was expected to take over as the top operating official at party headquarters, running its internal operations and its campaign and communication activities.

The only questions raised by this move were whether Richards should have been removed outright, and if his replacement, an ally of Vice President George Bush, was conservative enough to satisfy the extreme right wing of the party (he was not). There was no talk of the party's integrity being compromised or of a relatively independent national party and party headquarters, chiefly responsible to and representative of its grass-roots base. It was accepted that a president has the right to do as he pleases with the national party. This predicament reaffirmed that the national party and its staff are little more than extensions of the campaign arm of the White House. They have no independent identity, power, or representative function.

The situation is no different in the Democratic party. From day one as president, Jimmy Carter seemed intent on making clear this dependency. Carter's pollster Patrick Caddell proposed in a memo that the incoming administration act quickly to "Carterize" the Democratic National Committee and the national party and determine qualifications for the national chairman.

> It is clear that if the DNC [Democratic National Committee] is going to be "Carterized" and made a political wing of the White House, that requires a chairman who is a loyalist, and essentially a Carter

83

insider. I suspect that any move that brings in someone who has an independent constituency and other political interests is going to result in an inability of the DNC to really carry out the functions we need. I think that the DNC chairman's selection be along the lines of someone who is both a loyalist, an insider, and a person who is willing to take direction from the Governor's [Carter's] political and personal staff.[4]

The new chair appointed by Carter was Kenneth Curtis, a former governor of Maine and a personal friend of the president since the days when both served as chief executives of their respective states. Curtis was naive, though, in thinking that the national party was somewhat independent of the president. When he began complaining about the day-to-day meddling of White House political operatives in national committee affairs, the White House began disseminating stories to friendly media representatives concerning Curtis's "weak" leadership. Despite his popularity with party professionals, congressmen, state party leaders, and the media, Curtis was quickly replaced by a far more obliging national chair who was to prove his loyalty repeatedly in the events leading up to and including the 1980 prenomination race.

The Powers and Operations of the National Committees

On paper, the national committees have formidable powers. For example, the by-laws of the Democratic party charge its national party to—

- maintain a national party headquarters.

- conduct the national campaign for the party's presidential and vice-presidential nominees.

- assist in the election of all Democratic candidates in any general elections.

- promote party organization at all levels (which includes, according to *Rules*, political research, communications, media coverage, public relations, coordination of party levels and party and nonparty groups and leaders, speakers' activities, program initiation, performance of party mandates, and "the discharge and fulfillment by the Party of its platform pledges and commitments publicly made").

- encourage Democratic clubs.

- finance party activities (through state quotas among other things).

- arrange and manage the national committee.

- implement the national convention platform.

- "establish, maintain, and sponsor such committees, groups, staffs or councils for the formulation of Party policy not inconsistent with the platform of the National Convention."

- maintain sustaining party membership.

- do any and all other things reasonably incidental to the performance and exercise of the duties imposed and powers conferred by the National Convention in promoting the principles and programs of the Democratic Party.[5]

There are substantial, actual, and inferred powers in this list (which is not much different from the Republican National Committee's authorization), to which can be added the efforts of the Democratic party's reform movement to fashion a more vital, independent, and representative national party. These efforts resulted in a "party charter," allegedly akin to a party constitution, that attempted to redefine the national party's role and add to its responsibilities and prestige. For example, the party charter, adopted in 1976, called for—[6]

- a Judicial Council, much like a supreme court, to settle on an acceptable body of party law and to adjudicate intra-party squabbles, thus keeping them out of the federal and state courts.

- midterm party conferences, to establish a cohesive party policy in the off-years between presidential elections and to update the party platform, thus giving the party a cohesiveness and relevance to its policy commitments that had not existed before. The Democrats did hold midterm conferences in 1974, 1978, and 1982, which constituted a new departure for the national parties, but they did not quite fulfill their creators' hopes.

- a national finance council to fund national party operations.

- a National Education and Training Council to develop "education and training programs for the Democratic Party in furtherance of its objectives," an agency more familiar to the Social Democrats and other European parties.

However laudable the objectives of those who desire a strong national party presence tied to its long-run interests and more clearly responsive to its rank and file membership, in the present context these aims are visionary. The truth is that the national parties at present represent no independent constituencies to whom they should respond in order to best serve their own long-term survival needs. There is no sense that the national parties' best interests may transcend those of any one candidate or administration or that long-run interest is tied to the adequacy of the parties' performance at all levels and in each branch of government in representing its constituent base.

Functionally, the national committees exist as a centralized clearinghouse for the state parties and to organize and administer the quadrennial national conventions. Ultimately, they serve only as extensions of the White House, a relationship Ronald Reagan made clear and one that Jimmy Carter seemed to carry to extremes. Reagan and Carter are not the only presidents, of course, to see the national committees only in terms of how they can best serve their own interests. This is the common perception, held not only by presidents, but also by congressmen, governors, state and local politicians and party professionals of all levels. It is a view also held by the media.

This is not to say that within these limits a national committee might not be well organized and effective in mounting a series of operations. The Republican National Committee, for example, has excelled in recent years in raising substantial funds for a broad range of national party operations. The Democrats, however, outside of setting and enforcing rules in presidential selection, have yet to move significantly beyond the passive role that characterized the parties through most of the fifties and sixties. In fact, the Democratic National Committee has only recently paid off the debts it assumed after the 1968 presidential campaign, a burden that severely hampered any efforts to expand its organizational efforts.

It is possible for a national committee to assert itself more—assuming funding is available—in the periods in which the party does not control the White House. Again, the Republicans have been more successful than the Democrats at this type of party-building under the guidance of an assertative national committee directly concerned with the nuts and bolts of campaign management, candidate recruitment, and organizational resuscitation. The leadership shown by the Republican National Committee in both the periods 1976–1980 and 1964–1968 does indicate what a resourceful national party is capable of achieving.

▰▰▰ REASSESSING NATIONAL PARTY OPERATIONS AND RESOURCES

To this point, the critique of the national parties has been traditional, stressing their weak organization in cross-national comparative terms, their dependence on presidential goodwill, and their lack of any ties of consequence to the party's base. There is another perspective, however, that has been advanced in recent years. Essentially, what this school argues is that we may be witnessing a rebirth of the national parties. I am overstating the case—its arguments are far more cautious than this—but such a prospect could take place if some of the trends evident in the last few years take root. Those who take this point of view argue that there has been a decided turn toward nationalization and centralization of power, the two parties having taken different roads toward what is basically the same end.

The Democrats have stressed a redefinition of the rules governing national party autonomy and representation—most prominently manifested in the adoption of the party charter, a process it was previously argued that has *not* substantially increased their actual power in national politics—and a centralization of rule-making authority and interpretation over presidential selection at the national level. This has caused a decisive shift in the power to define the limits of presidential selection from state and local elected officials and party organizations to the national party leaders.[7] However, this surrender of power by the state parties has *not* served to reinforce the autonomy of the national parties from the White House (and, in fact, provides even greater incentive for a president to stage-manage the national committee and its subsidiary bodies, the "reform" commissions). The developing intraparty democratic features and decentralization of power found in presidential selection have *not* carried over into, or substantially affected, the traditional patterns of authority and decision-making within the national party organization.

87

The Republican party has taken a different road. Rather than an overt redefinition of the rules governing confederation of state parties under an umbrella national organization and with a minimal effort to restructure intraparty organizational arrangements, *the Republicans have made a serious effort to increase the functional importance of the national party* by making it more relevant to the consensus of the state and, to a more limited extent, local parties and to the concerns of Republican candidates seeking elective office. In this, the Republicans have been immensely successful.

Charles Longley nicely captures the conflicting party emphasis as well as sketching the concerns that prompted change and the potential implications a failure to further a strong party presence could bring:

> . . . the redefinition of national parties can be seen as an attempt by the parties to deal with changes in the electoral process. The national parties had become moribund; they were neither responsive nor resourceful . . . the party system was wrecking itself.
>
> The national party organizations have undergone a transformation. The Democratic party responded to systemic changes by emphasizing the necessity for intraparty democracy as a precondition for electoral effectiveness. The Republican Party has chosen to strengthen its national organizations through the provision of expanded services. That the two parties differ in the manifestation of their redefinition should not obscure what is in fact a remarkable transition from the era of "politics without power." In the absence of continued party redefinition, it can be argued that public policy will but reflect the objectives of self-styled "citizen action groups" or privately financed Political Action Committees, neither of which can profess to be more publicly responsible than political parties—themselves fragile vehicles for democracy.[8]

The Republican party at the national level has been more successful in responding to the visceral needs of a party system in trouble and its efforts have borne more immediate fruit. As a consequence, it is more instructive to inquire in greater depth about the changes it has instituted.

Cornelius P. Cotter and John F. Bibby argue that the national parties have been moving toward increased "institutionalization." By this, they mean

> . . . a process involving changing roles of party chairman, national committee members, and staff; the development of staff continuity; the elaboration of programmatic activity and division of labor; the development of regular financing; and rule elaboration. The critical dimension . . . is the development of the national party headquarters as agencies that have sufficient autonomy to enable them to define and pursue their own programs, *with assurance that their continued existence does not depend upon the whim of a presidential candidate or party chairman.*[9] (Emphasis added.)

This would seem a minimal definition of party independence and continuity (i.e., an organizational existence that cannot be terminated by a given candidate or president) and it is reasonable to assume that both national parties have arrived at such a position. Under only the most extreme circumstances—ones that are presently difficult to imagine—could one, or both, national party headquarters be closed. In the past—and the recent past for the Democrats, because of funding concerns—this was less unlikely. Historically, on many occasions the national parties did not have a home, an active national chairperson, a staff, or a budget. Nonetheless, the weight of historical developments has been toward an increased institutionalization of the national party and an acceptance of a stronger national party presence in areas once reserved by the states.

By itself, this does not represent the heart of the argument behind the reassertion of a national party presence. It is believed that there has been an elaboration of functions and "a broadening and diversifying of the national committee constituency away from exclusively presidential concerns. As the national committees move to regionalize their offices, maintain staff in the field, and provide services to state party organizations, it is likely that they will develop a firmer base of grass-roots support."[10] The trend is best exemplified by developments within the Republican party that occurred between the years 1976–1980. The Republicans substantially increased their revenues, provided a wide range of professional services to the state parties and to candidates, and 89 invested considerable amounts of money in state and local party organizations and elective races.

The Republican party's National Finance Committee reported in 1981 that it had increased its fund-raising 240 percent between 1976 and 1980. For these four years alone, it brought in $107.3 million, a record unmatched in party annals. The breakdown by year is as follows:[12]

▪ Year	▪ Amount Raised
1976	$19,000,000
1977	$10,700,000
1978	$14,500,000
1979	$17,100,000
1980	$46,000,000

The Democrats, allegedly the party of the "common man," concentrate on the "fat cats" for their money. About 67 percent of Democratic funds come from those able to give $100 or more. Eighty percent of Republican funds were contributed by people who gave less than $100.[12] The Republican National Committee, between 1979 and 1980 alone, almost doubled the number of direct mail contributors (up from 650,000 to 1.2 million). It also coordinated its direct mail program with the Republican House and Senate campaign committees. The total raised for the campaign was $7.2 million, roughly 75 percent of which went for operational costs. Yet the Republican National Committee enrolled 400,000 new sustaining members (twice what it had before), who should provide a continuing source of campaign revenue.[13]

The money was spent wisely. The National Finance Committee reported—

1. contributing $4.6 million, the maximum allowed under law, directly to the Reagan-Bush presidential campaign.

2. funding a $9.4 million advertising campaign on behalf of Republican candidates. As the Committee acknowledged, "during the last 16 days before election day, we ran this television campaign at the same pace as both major presidential candidates' television advertising . . . in effect, . . . giving us two nationwide election campaigns while the Democrats were operating only one."[14]

TABLE 7.2 ■ Expenditures by Democratic and Republican National Party Organizations in the 1980 Elections

Organization	Democratic ($)	Republican ($)
National committees	14,909,724	71,013,779
Congressional committees	2,038,401	25,690,935
Senatorial committees	1,618,162	21,920,337
Total	18,566,287	118,625,051

Source: Federal Election Commission as reported in Kenneth Janda, "Let's Have a Party," a paper delivered at the Annual Meeting of the Illinois Political Science Association, 1981.

3.   providing $3.2 million to U.S. Senate, House, gubernatorial, and state legislative candidates.[15]

Kenneth Janda analyzed the spending patterns of the major parties in the 1980 presidential election and found that the Republicans outspent the Democrats by $100 million![16] (Table 7.2)

The money not used directly in the 1980 campaign was plowed back into party operations. The results were impressive. An organizational revolution of sorts took place within the Republican party at the national level. Janda reports that prior to creation of the Local Elections Campaign Division, voter profiles of districts, seminars held for candidates, and campaign assistance, the Republicans in 1974 had lost 692 state legislative seats (a result of Nixon's resignation and Watergate). In 1976, they won back only twelve of these. In 1978, with the new local campaign emphasis, they captured 307 state legislative seats and in 1980 added another 271 seats.[17] These impressive gains resulted directly from the organizational emphasis, systematic funding initiatives, and improved service capabilities of the national committee.

Electoral successes are not the only indicator of the change in the Republican approach. There has also emerged a greater interdependence among Republican organizations at all levels, an increasing coherence to party structures, and a unification of efforts to seek mutually acceptable objectives (essentially electing Republicans at all levels to public office). The national party has attempted to achieve such goals by making itself more of a force in general election campaigns and by substantially upgrading its capabilities as a resource and funding source better able to serve state party and candidate needs.

Is this enough? Once the presidency has been won and the perpetual fear of extinction has been, once again, laid to rest, won't the national party sink again into the lethargy and subservience to the president that has all too often characterized both parties' role on the national scene?

There has been a consistent incremental change toward greater national authority in party affairs, a more stable and bureaucratic party presence, and an increased professionalism in both parties at the national level. But the real question is: Whose interest will these developments serve? Will they lead to a more representative and responsive party system? Or will the national parties simply prepare themselves to better execute their presidential master's wishes? Put another way, can the Democratic model, best symbolized by its objectives of a grass-roots representative party, and the Republican model, seen in its functional contributions to basic party concerns (i.e., winning office), be successfully crossbred? If so, there may be hope for the party system.

CHAPTER 8

Parties
at
the
State
Level

■

Relatively little is known about the operation and organization of state parties because of the enormous differences among them in policy-making, structure, and influence on elections. In attempting to capture and explain this variability, we have yet to seriously develop the contextual, environmental, and institutional factors that set the limits for party operations, much less compare and explain their success (or lack of it). Some recent research does hold promise for initially understanding the role played by the state party organizations and it is these studies that we will largely focus on.

There have been many studies of political parties in individual states, although little of a comparative nature exists and not much can be extracted even from the limited comparative works that identify the essence of the state operations. As a consequence, assessing what the state parties do, how they are structured, and what contributions they make to governance has been difficult. Even today, much of the research is in the process of being analyzed. What we do have, for the most part, are preliminary and fragmented studies. The strength of the works that will be cited is that they represent more than has been available in the past and address the more relevant and least investigated questions concerning the state parties and their political import.

██████ CLASSIFYING STATE PARTIES BY THE COMPETITIVE PATTERN OF THE STATES

It is difficult to rank or compare state parties. One method, based on the work of V. O. Key, Jr., is to categorize state parties in relation to the factional patterns evident in their politics.[1] Malcolm E. Jewell and David N. Olson have demarcated three types:[2]

1. Cohesive parties, or those able to resolve internal factional rivalries to the point that the party presents a unified front in elections. Such parties can range from machine-type organizations, to southern party oligarchies (the Byrd machine in Virginia), to relatively open and participant-oriented parties such as the Democratic-Farmer-Labor party of Minnesota.

2. Bifactional parties, or those dominated by two major factions, each with differing perspectives and each proposing and supporting alternative candidate slates. The factionalism that is normally of long-standing duration can center on regional differences, a liberal-conservative split, personalities, or antagonistic social groups within the coalition.

3. Multifactional parties, the most commonly found type of state party system, or those lacking internal cohesion and suffering from severe fragmentation among the groups, issues, and candidates that seek the party's endorsement. In such cases, the party itself is more like an umbrella organization, virtually impotent in terms of exercising an independent control over the priorities and disputes that rage among its factions. The parties themselves can be liberal or conservative and can be identified with any region of the country. For example, within the Democratic party both the California Democrats and the Texas Democrats are considered to be multifactional, as are, within the Republican party, the New York and Kentucky Republicans (Table 8.1).

Using these categories, Jewell and Olson have classified state parties according to the competitive status of the party system. These range from one-party dominant state political cultures (excluding southern Democratic parties) through "majority" party states (where both parties compete consistently and there is some turnover in office, although one party normally wins) to highly competitive states in which the party suffers a quasi-permanent

TABLE 8.1 ■ Classification of State Parties by Factionalism and Competitiveness

Competitive Status of Party	Factional Pattern					
	Cohesive	Bifactional		Multifactional		
I. Dominant						
Democratic	Va. 1930–65	Tex. 1950s, 1960s La. 1940s Ga. 1930–1960		Ala. Ark. Ga. La.	Miss. S.C. Tex.	
II. Majority:						
Democratic	— Hawaii			Fla. Ky. Md. Mo. N.Mex.	N.C. Okla. R.I. Tenn. W.Va.	
Republican	Colo. Vt.	N.H.		S.Dak. Wyo.		
III. Competitive						
Democratic	Del. Iowa N.Dak.	Ind. Kans. Minn. Mont. Utah		Alaska Ariz. Calif. Conn. Idaho Ill.	Maine Mass. Mich. Neb. Nev. N.J. N.Y.	Ohio Oreg. Pa. Va. Wash. Wis.
Republican	Del. Ind. Nev. N.J. Ohio Utah Va.	Ariz. Idaho Ill. Iowa Kans.	Mass. Mich. Minn Mont. Wash. Wis.	Alaska Calif. Conn. Maine	Neb. N.Y. N.Dak. Oreg. Pa.	
IV. Minority						
Democratic	Colo.	Vt.		N.H. S.Dak. Wyo.		
Republican	R.I. W.Va.	Md. Mo. N.Mex.	N.C. Okla. Tenn.	Fla. Hawaii Ky.		
V. Electorally combative:						
Republican	La.	Ala. Ark. Miss.		Ga. S.C. Tex.		

Source: Malcolm E. Jewell and David M. Olson, *American State Political Parties and Elections*, revised edition, Homewood, Ill.: Dorsey, 1982.

minority status (the other side of the majority party category) and "electorally combative" party systems (states in which a badly outgunned minority party nonetheless contests elections to the extent it can and with occasional success, i.e., the Republicans in the South).

The problem with this type of analysis is that, while helpful in sorting through the maze of alternative state types, its analytic possibilities are limited. The categories of party cohesion are so broad that there is little common ground from which to reduce and identify the factors that explain the new strain of party system that has developed, its permutations, and its future course. Table 8.1 illustrates the difficulties. When the 50 states and 100 parties shown in the table are cross-classified by cohesion (factionalism and competition), fifteen possible types of state party emerge. While such an approach has a descriptive utility, and this is how Jewell and Olson employ it, and while it does impose an order and understanding on the variety of individual state party types, it cannot be taken much further.

◼◼◼ CLASSIFYING STATE PARTIES BY STRUCTURE AND OPERATIONS

Possibly more promising is the field research into state party organizations undertaken in recent years by a team of political scientists, including Cornelius P. Cotter, John F. Bibby, James L. Gibson, and Robert J. Huckshorn. They have attempted to identify the institutional dimensions unique to the state parties and then to develop from these indices structural attributes that can be used to measure campaign effectiveness, policy formulation impact, and the interaction between party and political environment.[3] The research is ongoing but enough is available to begin a mapping of the state party organizations, their present status, and, to an extent, trends in their evolution over time.

Cotter et al. ranked the states on two dimensions: the restrictiveness or laxity of statutory regulations governing parties and the public statutory support given the parties (supportive state laws, for example, protect the party's control over its nominating process and can provide campaign subsidies to the parties or their candidate).

The state rankings on the two indices did not correlate highly. Also, the presumption was that there would be a strong relation-

TABLE 8.2 ■ Characteristics of State Party Chairs, 1980

Characteristics	All Parties	Republican	Democratic
Percent full–time employed as chair	29.4	28.9	30.0
Percent salaried as chair	23.9	27.0	20.0
Mean years active in politics	19.7	18.6	21.2
Mean years state chair	2.5	2.1	3.1
Mean hours worked per week (non-election year)	24.9	26.6	22.6
Mean hours worked per week (election year)	36.3	36.7	35.8

Source: William Crotty, "Political Financing and State Party Organizational Effectiveness," a paper prepared for delivery at the International Political Science Association Meeting, Rio de Janeiro, 1982.

ship between regulatory and facilitative state attitudes toward the parties and party organizational strength. This did not occur. What the researchers did find was a relationship between pro-party state statutes and party organization strength over time (1960–1978). A facilitative state posture was associated with a measurable strengthening of the organizations of both the parties, although the relationship was not strong.[4]

Such analyses begin to define the legal environment in which the parties operate and the manner in which state political cultures affect the parties' structures and operations.

The state parties do appear to have become increasingly bureaucratic. An examination of the state parties at three points in time (1960–1964, 1970–1974, and 1979–1980) shows an increase in the proportion with full-time state chairs. Also, by 1980 virtually all of the state parties sampled (90 percent) in the Cotter study had at least one full-time executive (the state chair or an executive director). The salary of the state chairs rose 180 percent over the twenty year period.[5]

Another study of state party operations in 1980 examined the organizational status of state parties (Table 8.2).[6] It found that most state chairs worked close to full time in election years and also put in a good number of hours in non-election years. State chairs experience a high turnover on the average, which suggests their tie-in to the outcome of gubernatorial elections (the winning candidate normally chose his own chair) and that the position may have enough prestige to be seen as desirable within the context of 97

TABLE 8.3 ■ Percent of Role Orientations of State Party Chairs, 1980

Role	All Parties	Republican	Democratic
Party image building	78.8/22.8[a]	73.0/21.5	86.2/24.7
Criticizing other party	43.9/10.6	54.1/11.4	41.4/ 9.6
Party campaigning	76.1/16.7	71.1/16.2	82.8/17.4
Party fund raising	79.1/23.2	81.6/22.4	75.9/24.2
Party administration	79.1/25.8	76.3/27.6	82.8/23.2

Source: William Crotty, "Political Financing and State Party Organizational Effectiveness," a paper prepared for delivery at the International Political Science Association Meeting, Rio de Janeiro, 1982.
[a] The first number of each pair is the percent of party chairs saying given activity is very important. The second number is the mean percentage of the time spent by state chairs on that activity.

state politics. The more sought after it is, the more likely it is to have a high rate of turnover.

In terms of role orientations, the study of state parties in the 1980 election year indicated that state chairs see fund-raising, party administration, image-building (public relations), and campaigning among the most significant of their duties (Table 8.3). Fund-raising, administration, and image-building consume more than 70 percent of their time. There are differences between the parties—the Democrats put more effort into campaigning and less into attacking the opposition than do Republicans—but the general tendencies are the same.

The 1980 study also showed that both parties concentrated on providing candidates with campaign services, neglecting local and county contests in favor of state-level races, and becoming only moderately involved in congressional campaigns (Table 8.4).

Beyond assisting in campaigns, state party services to candidates are limited (Tables 8.4 and 8.5). Both parties make some effort to help fund campaigns, the Republican state parties providing such backup services as research assistances, policy papers, and speakers. The Democratic state parties are considerably less active in these regards.

Several other trends in state party operations are also noteworthy. Cotter and his associates report that between the years 1959–1961 and 1979–1980, the average budget for a state party increased from $100,000 to better than $350,000 and the percentage of state parties whose financial resources could be classified as either competitive or high rose from 45 percent to 70 percent.[7]

The data on state parties in 1980 reveal two things of consequence in regard to increased budgets: first, that the budgeting

TABLE 8.4 ■ Services Provided by State Party to Candidates for Public Office[a]

Services	All Parties	Republican	Democratic
Advice on campaigning	76.1	81.6	69.0
Research assistance on policy and/or opponents	49.3	63.2	31.0
Speakers	28.4	42.1	10.3
Assistance in planning T.V. and radio presentations	31.8	36.8	25.0
Provision of campaign literature, films, etc.	30.3	31.6	28.6
Funds for campaign	46.2	47.4	44.4

Source: William Crotty, "Political Financing and State Party Organizational Effectiveness," a paper prepared for delivery at the International Political Science Association Meeting, Rio de Janeiro, 1982.
[a] Percentage reporting "usually."

for election and non-election years, if not ample, appears to be greater than many had anticipated, a confirmation of the findings in the over-time analyses of state parties; and second, in a trend that is found repeatedly, the Republican state parties do far better than do the Democratic ones (Table 8.6). The average budget for all parties is roughly $400,000 in election years. The differences between the parties are substantial, however. Republican state party budgets are more than $200,000 higher in election years and $160,000 higher in non-election years than those of the Democrats.[8]

Overall, an analysis of the Cotter data also shows that the budgets of state parties (measured in constant dollars) and state party headquarters' staffing have increased substantially during the

TABLE 8.5 ■ Degree of Activity of State Party in Elections for Public Office[a]

Race	All Parties	Republican	Democratic
Governor	73.4	67.6	81.5
State Legislature	80.0	89.2	67.9
U.S. Congress, House	42.4	31.6	57.1
U.S. Senate	46.9	36.1	60.7
County Offices	6.3	11.1	22.2
Local (city/town) offices	6.1	10.5	17.9

Source: William Crotty, "Political Financing and State Party Organizational Effectiveness," a paper prepared for delivery at the International Political Science Association Meeting, Rio de Janeiro, 1982.
[a] Percentage reporting "very active."

TABLE 8.6 ■ State Party Budget, 1980[a]

Party	Election Year ($)	Non–Election Year ($)
All state parties	398,333	275,557
Republican	487,250	343,556
Democrats	279,778	177,640

Source: William Crotty, "Political Financing and State Party Organizational Effectiveness," a paper prepared for delivery at the International Political Science Association Meeting, Rio de Janeiro, 1982.

[a] Mean operating budget.

period 1960–1980, positive signs in the overall movement toward a greater level of party institutionalization at the state level. There are sharp party and regional differences, however, in the nature of the developments.

Republicans have always been better financed than Democrats. On the average, during the 1960–1980 period, the northern Republican parties—the most lavishly financed of the state parties—spent between $175,000 and $190,000 more than the Democrats, northern or southern. The northern Republicans maintained their substantial advantage while northern Democrats, if anything, saw their financial resources decline over these two decades, although both southern Republicans and southern Democrats had more available money than the northern Democratic parties. Needless to say, southern Republican parties were better financed than southern Democratic ones.

In terms of staffing, the Republican state parties do better than the Democratic state parties. Again, the northern Republican state parties are well ahead of the other state parties and have better than double the staff available to the Democratic state parties. The northern Democrats are in about the same place they were two decades ago. The other three categories of state party—northern Republicans, southern Republicans, and southern Democrats (which had virtually no staffing available in 1960)—have demonstrated substantial improvement over the years.

A few differences are clear. The Republican state parties are considerably better funded and staffed than are their Democratic counterparts and while, overall, there has been a move toward more institutionalized parties at the state level, the non-southern Democratic parties sampled in the Cotter study show little, if any, improvement.

The 1980 state party data indicate that state party leaders consider their parties to be "fairly well organized"[9] (Table 8.7). About

TABLE 8.7 ■ Extent of State Party Organization, 1980

Degree of Organization	All Parties (%)	Republican (%)	Democratic (%)
Highly organized	5.9	2.6	10.0
Well organized	27.9	28.9	26.7
Fairly well organized	44.1	44.7	43.3
Poorly organized	22.1	23.7	20.0
Not organized state-wide	0	0	0
Mean number of party staff	8	11	5

Source: William Crotty, "Political Financing and State Party Organizational Effectiveness," a paper prepared for delivery at the International Political Science Association Meeting, Rio de Janeiro, 1982.

one-third of the state parties consider themselves to be very well organized and in 1980 Republican state party staffs outnumbered the Democrats by a 2:1 ratio.

Both parties do relatively well when it comes to the degree of control and interaction between state party leaders and other party officials and elective office-holders (Table 8.8). State chairs appear to meet regularly with other state party officials and with county and local party representatives out contact with national party officials is far more limited. State party leaders do not interact with any degree of frequency with public officeholders at the county or local levels but they do, in contrast, meet with state legislators, in particular, with members of the state's delegation to the Congress (a more pronounced tendency for Democrats), and with state-level administrators (Table 8.8). Overall, and with the exception of contacts with the national party, the degree of intraorganizational communication and coherence appears to be good.

■■■■ SUMMARY MEASURES OF THE STATE PARTIES OVER TIME

A number of the indicators used in the Cotter, Bibby, Gibson, and Huckshorn studies have been combined into more generalized   101

TABLE 8.8 ■ Degree of Contact of State Party Chairs with Party Officials and Public Office-Holders[a]

	All Parties	Republican	Democratic
Party Officials and Workers			
Local party officials	59.1	51.4	69.0
County party congressional district officials	62.5	61.1	64.3
Other state party officials	84.8	86.5	82.8
National party officials	24.2	21.6	27.6
Public Office-Holders			
Local government office-holders	18.2	16.2	20.7
County government office-holders	10.8	8.1	14.3
State administrative office-holders	43.1	41.7	44.8
State legislators	65.2	62.2	69.0
U.S. senators and representatives	48.5	43.2	55.2

Source: William Crotty, "Political Financing and State Party Organizational Effectiveness," a paper prepared for delivery at the International Political Science Association Meeting, Rio de Janeiro, 1982.
[a] Percentage reporting frequent contact.

measures of state party institutionalization. These have been defined by Cotter and his associates to include three component parts:[10]

1. "bureaucratization" of the state party's headquarters (continuity of operations, divisions of labor, financing, and professionalization of leadership positions);

2. "programmatic" activity of the state party, which includes institutional support (fund raising, servicing local parties, electoral mobilization, polling, issue concerns, and state party publications) and candidate-directed activities (candidate and convention delegate recruitment, preprimary endorsements, and financial and service contributions to candidates); and

3. rules of "complexity," a measure of the presence, accessibility, and comprehensiveness of party rules governing party officers and based on the assumption that the greater the elaboration of codes for party behavior, the greater the institutionalization of the party.

Combining these three dimensions should provide one measure of a state party's "institutionalization."

While the scoring of each indicator is too complicated to review here, the nature of the differences among the state parties in various regions is easy enough to discern. There are significant differences between the two major parties and, within the parties, between those in southern and nonsouthern states. On the measures of bureaucratization and programmatic activity and on the summary index of institutionalization, the ordering of the parties, from strongest to weakest, is consistently northern Republican state parties, southern Republican state parties, northern Democratic state parties, and southern Democratic state parties. In relation to the elaboration of rules within the parties, the Democrats—reflecting their recent brush with the reform movement within their party (which mandates that such rules be made available)—are slightly ahead of the northern Republicans. Southern Republican state parties have the least formalized codes to govern intraparty behavior, a reflection of both the newness of these organizations and the lack of any clear directives from the national party requiring their adoption. In general, on all the significant indicators, including the composite measure of institutionalization, the Republican state parties, north and south, are better organized and more active than are the Democratic state parties.

A developed party structure correlates with electoral success, although which comes first is uncertain. The Democratic Party's generations of experience in one-party southern states, its situation in such pro-Democratic northern strongholds as Massachusetts, and both parties' structures in California seem to affirm that there is no intrinsic reason why electoral success should lead to a strong party organization. More than likely, an increasingly vital party organization contributes to a better electoral showing.

In a related study of the campaign services provided to candidates, Robert W. Biersack and Patricia Haeuser, using the same data base as Cotter, et al., found that the institutionalized, bureaucratic development of the state parties did correspond to their ability and willingness to provide campaign management services and resources to candidates.[11] The more institutionalized the state party, the more likely it was to engage in these activities, which comes as no surprise. More unexpected—and more encouraging to those who believe that parties will have to adapt to the realities of television and the new age of campaigning to survive—was the nature of the campaign services offered. Party organization was less related to performance of traditional party activities, specifically voter mobilization and election day drives, than expected. The state parties did offer more candidate training seminars, public opinion polling, campaign advertising, and media counseling—

all staples of the "new politics"—than had previously been realized.[12]

If these findings are correct, it may be that state parties are not simply extending their traditional services, but are developing new and relevant resources consistent with the need to adapt to a changing political environment. This conclusion is more optimistic than the data presented in the studies mentioned would warrant. Still, it remains a possibility. If true, it bodes well for the future of political parties, at least at the state level.

■■■■ CONCLUSION

State parties are reasonably well organized. They have increased their organizational development and sophistication over time and, when organized and funded, they are willing to invest heavily and meaningfully in election campaigns, thus better fulfilling the traditional assumptions of what a party's role should be. In general, Republicans—at both the national and state levels—are considerably better organized and funded than the Democrats and are more active in campaigns. Overall, should these findings hold up, it appears that the state parties are in much better shape than had been assumed and, should the trends outlined continue, will be in even better shape in the future. It is reasonable then to expect state parties to assert an increasingly influential role in state politics, thus becoming significant force within the national party system.

All of this may come to pass but for now it is sufficient to know that state parties are adequately organized, vital institutions that appear to play a significant role (though one that is still far from being totally clear) in the politics of their respective states. Before the wave of recent studies, this was more than most would have thought to be the case.

The actual impact parties at the state level make on campaigns, on policy-making, and in mobilizing votes and electing candidates is not clear. Do they really make a difference? If so, what explains the conditions under which they have a maximum or minimum impact? How much worse off, and in what ways, would we be if parties did not exist (or if they failed to operate with any degree of efficiency)? Such questions have yet to be asked, much less answered, in any serious manner by any researchers.

CHAPTER 9

Local Parties

L ocal parties and party organizations are even more varied than state parties and, if anything, even less understood. There are a scattering of localized case studies that describe either one party in a given area, the activists within a local party organization and their politically relevant views and backgrounds, or given campaigns. These studies are difficult to integrate and provide only rough insights into local parties and their operations.[1]

■ NONPARTISAN ELECTIONS

The sheer size of the task involved in assessing the enormous diversity of local party types is an obvious deterrent to any full-scale research effort. But there is another reason as well: the nonpartisan nature of most local elections. Approximately two-thirds (64 percent) of the almost three thousand cities in the United States with a population of over 5,000 employ some form of nonpartisan electoral systems (Table 9.1). Virtually all cities in the West favor this type of election as do most of the cities in the South, the border states, and the Midwest. Nonpartisan municipal elections are less common along the Atlantic seaboard and in the older cities long organized along partisan political lines. They are in a distinct minority in the states that stretch from Maryland to New York. 105

TABLE 9.1 ■ Characteristics of Cities Using Nonpartisan Elections

Classification	No. of Cities Reporting (A)	Cities Having Nonpartisan Elections	
		No.	% of (A)
Total, all cities	4008	2813	70.2
Population group			
Over 1,000,000	3	2	66.7
500,000–1,000,000	12	9	75.0
250,000– 499,999	24	16	66.7
100,000– 249,999	93	69	74.2
50,000– 99,999	223	159	71.3
25,000– 49,999	458	322	70.3
10,000– 24,999	993	663	66.8
5,000– 9,999	1026	697	67.9
2,500– 4,999	1176	876	74.5
Geographic division			
New England	187	101	54.0
Mid-Atlantic	611	69	11.3
East North Central	839	540	64.4
West North Central	456	421	92.3
South Atlantic	546	484	88.6
East South Central	237	180	75.9
West South Central	438	373	85.2
Mountain	216	182	84.3
Pacific Coast	478	463	96.9
Form of government			
Mayor-council	2042	1191	58.3
Council-manager	1854	1540	83.1
Commission	112	82	73.2

Source: *Municipal Yearbook, 1982.*

A nonpartisan election is one in which political parties are barred by law from competing and in which party symbols and labels cannot appear on the ballot. If it does nothing else, an examination of nonpartisan elections emphasizes how relevant the political parties are to the democratic enterprise.

The Case for Nonpartisan Elections

Corruption, inefficiency, machine politics, big city ethnic populations, and the changing conception of government from aloof manager to social service provider supported the Progressive Movement's desire in the early 1900s to eliminate the party presence from elections. The president of Cornell University put the matter bluntly:

Without the slightest exaggeration we may assert
that, with very few exceptions, the city governments
of the United States are the worst in Christendom—
the most expensive, the most inefficient, and the most
corrupt. No one who has any considerable knowledge
of our own country and of other countries can deny
this. . . .

What is the cause of the difference between
municipalities in the old world and in the new? I do
not allow that their populations are better than ours.
What accounts, then, for the better municipal
development in their case and for the miserable results
in our own? My answer is this: we are attempting to
govern our cities upon a theory which has never been
found to work practically in any part of the
world. . . .

What is this evil theory? It is simply that the city
is a political body: that its interior affairs have to do
with national parties and issues. My fundamental
contention is that a city is a corporation: that as a city
it has nothing to do with general political interests;
that party political names and duties are utterly out of
place there. The questions in a city are not political
questions. . . . The work of a city being the creation
and control of the city property, it should logically be
managed as a piece of property of those who have
created it, who have a title to it, or a real substantial
part in it, and who can therefore feel strongly their
duty to it. Under our theory that a city is a political
nobody, a crowd of illiterate peasants, freshly raked
in from Irish bogs, or Bohemian mines, or Italian
robber nests, may exercise virtual control. How such
men govern cities, we know too well; as a rule they
are not alive even to their own most direct
interests. . . .

We . . . are putting ourselves upon a basis which
has always failed and will always fail—the idea that a
city is a political body, and therefore that it is to be
ruled, in the long run, by a city proletarian mob,
obeying national party cries.[2]

Such beliefs led to two basic assumptions: first, that politicians
and political parties could not be trusted; and, second, that the 107

principles of "efficient business administration" could be applied to the management of civic affairs. Politics, in short, should be taken out of city politics. Not an easy thing to do as it turns out, and one with unforeseen, and largely undesirable, consequences.

In actuality, the nonpartisan movement—as radical and unrealistic as it may seem in retrospect—was not out of line with dominant themes in the American political psyche. As William Goodman observed: "The Progressives' attacks upon party organization were undertaken on behalf of the *real* American principles, not on behalf of a new set of alien principles. Neither within the party cadres nor generally among the leaders of reform was there any disposition to radicalize the political system."[3] Robert Ward, developing the historical antecedents of these "*real* American principles," has written that "nonpartisanship harks back to the traditional concept of local government, to Jefferson's high expectations for the rational capacity of the yeoman, and to that strand in American political reasoning that relies on unfettered individualism."[4]

Little wonder that with the impetus provided by machine corruption and the abuse of political office and with a set of reform proposals calling on emotional commitments that had, in fact, helped shaped the American dream of democracy, nonpartisan elections, once introduced, caught on quickly. They soon emerged as the dominant form of municipal contests. As Table 9.1 indicates, nonpartisan elections dominate in suburbs and in cities of all sizes, and are especially prominent in medium-sized cities (those in the 250,000 to 500,000 population range) and in those cities that have adopted a council-manager form of government, another Progressive Era proposal. In all, while slightly less than two-thirds of the cities with a population of over 5,000 people have nonpartisan electoral systems, 88 percent of those with less than 5,000 people also employed nonpartisan elections.

Critics would argue that nonpartisan elections have resulted in—[5]

- greater citizen apathy at the local level.

- lower voter turnouts than for partisan elections.

- less competitive political races.

- a magnification of the incumbent's advantage in an election. Always significant, it is maximized in a system that deemphasizes organized opposition and the availability of citizen information.

- protest voting, which is difficult to focus, thwarted.

- a lessening of political accountability, in the absence of a party presence that can be held responsible for abuses of office or failures to enact promises.

- campaigns that are less serious, less issue-oriented, and more trivial. Pressing civic issues are less likely to be publicly debated in nonpartisan campaigns and it is less likely that they will be resolved directly through elections.

- declines in the levels of voter information. Without the political parties to educate the public to the basic issues confronting the government, the alternative solutions, the nature of the offices being sought and their limitations, and the candidates and their qualifications, there is less relevant information available to the voter and the consequence is a less informed citizenry.

- less involvement by, and less representation for, lower socioeconomic groups. The electorate tends to be confined to the middle-class, better educated, higher income groups with the skills necessary to overcome the informational, legal (e.g., registration), and attitudinal restraints on participation.

- a Republican bias to election systems. Such elections work to the advantage of the groups that support Republican candidates and policies and to the disadvantage of those who normally identify with and support Democratic candidates and positions.

- political power (in the absence of political parties) passing to other organized groups (or communications outlets) with the ability to seek out candidates, fund electoral races, mobilize support, and communicate with the city's electorate. These would include: civic organizations, the Chamber of Commerce, labor unions, newspapers and local television outlets, ad hoc citizens' committees, de facto parties (the "Good Citizen" party or "Save Our Schools" coalitions), fraternal orders, women's clubs, civic improvement associations, athletic organizations, social clubs, and even church groups. 109

- the negation of cue-giving, the device through which the parties, by conferring their labels ("Democratic" or "Republican") on candidates, provide voters with a convenient framework for organizing their political worlds and, in the absence of more compelling information, for making their electoral choices.

- the atrophy of local party organizations. Denied the opportunity to compete, local parties disintegrate, weakening the grass-roots base of the political parties nationally and restricting the identification and recruitment of future potential party and public officeholders.

- an overemphasis on name identification and "trivial" qualities in deciding among candidates. Fred I. Greenstein argues that "*anything* that makes a candidate's name stand out may be to his advantage"[6] in a situation where the individuals are largely unknown, the nonpartisan ballot is confusing, the parties are not available to focus concerns, and voters do not have opinions on local issues. And even when voters have taken positions on policy matters, there is limited information available on where the many candidates stand on the issues. Building on the work of Charles R. Adrian and others, Greenstein has suggested that in such situations the following factors assume unusual importance in voter decision-making:[7]

  1. Celebrity status. A well-known athlete, civic leader, or news commentator (actually anyone with name recognition) has the advantage.

  2. Name association. Having the same name as someone else who is famous in politics can help. At one time, there was a rash of "John F. Kennedys" running for and winning elective office all over America.

  3. Ballot position. Candidates at the top of the ballot gain more votes, as do those at the very bottom. Voter fatigue penalizes those in the middle.

  4. Ethnicity. People tend to vote for names—Irish, Italian, German, Polish, WASP—that they believe at least share the same ethnic and cultural roots and values that they do, a dangerous assumption in a land where names are often anglicized or changed by marriage and divorce or for a variety of personal, legal, or business reasons.

All in all, nonpartisan elections may not represent the best way to decide who should rule or how the most important issues facing a locality should be resolved.

However much the experts may differ, it appears that non-partisan elections, in comparison to partisan elections, provide less of what is expected of political campaigns, political representation, and political accountability. These liabilities may be such that in any long-run perspective they prove more of a deterrent than a benefit to the democratic enterprise.

Many of the arguments that arose to justify nonpartisan electoral arrangements and, to an extent, that are put forward today on their behalf are more arguments against weaknesses in the party system than arguments explicitly favoring nonpartisanship, i.e., apolitical politics, which is an impossibility.

Willis D. Hawley takes the stand that "most all politics is dominated by the action of organized groups and *the only issue is whether parties should be among those groups*."[8] (Emphasis added.) He quotes Samuel Huntington on the subject to good effect:

> . . . the development of a strong party substitutes an institutionalized public interest for fragmented private ones. The evils attributed to party are, in reality, the attributes of a disorganized and fragmented politics of clique and faction which prevails when parties are nonexistent or still very weak. Their cure lies in political organization.[9]

Nonpartisan elections take the failings of political parties to extremes. A more useful response to the weaknesses of urban parties would be to emphasize improvement in their operational and representative capabilities. Effective politics is group politics, and the most significant and forceful organizers of conflicting group interests have been the political parties. Without them, there is chaos, which only reinforces voter lack of interest and noninvolvement in politics. Political decision-making, as a result, is confined to a small group of officeholders responsible, at best, to a relatively narrow segment of the electorate.

The choice is between the anarchy of laissez-faire nonpartisanship—with its indisputable policy and political consequences—and the organized combat of the political parties, whatever their failings.

111

■■■ PARTIES IN AN URBAN SETTING

A basic knowledge of local parties, their membership, and their work within a community is not readily available. Many of the studies done on urban areas are anecdotal or biographical, focusing on colorful local political figures and their exploits. There are limited case studies of party operations or personnel in given areas, but their restricted time frame and narrow focus make generalizing from their findings risky. However, there has been comparative research on political parties in an urban setting that has begun to develop a relevant data base for the study of local parties. The findings are suggestive.[10] The study examined party operations in five major urban areas: Chicago, Detroit, Los Angeles, Houston and Nashville.

The researchers (who included Samuel J. Eldersveld, Dwaine Marvick, Richard Murray and Kent Tedin, and Anne Hopkins) developed a related set of problems they intended to address; they employed a comparable questionnaire, modified for use in the relevant localities; they focused on related target populations—precinct or ward committeemen or their functional equivalents, the group closest to the voter and presumed to know how active the party and other political groups would be in their immediate areas during the election; and they concentrated on examining the same time frame and local party effort during the 1980 presidential campaign and election.

Based on these data, limited comparisons can be made of relevance to the understanding of the operations of political parties in urban areas.

The cities examined cover a range of political types: Chicago is an old machine city fairly typical of the big city, ethnic-based party organizations of the large industrialized states of the northeast and Midwest. Detroit is roughly similar in background, but with a more strongly organized union element. There is one other significant contrast: neither Detroit nor any other American city of any size in recent times has had a powerful political organization comparable to the Chicago–Cook County Democrats. Machine politics and Chicago are virtually synonymous. Detroit has an ethnic, blue collar base similar to those of many of the struggling cities in the north. Los Angeles, on the other hand, is noted for being less reliant on the traditional party organizations, common in the East and upper Midwest, and more attuned to television and the "new politics" of the media age. Nashville is a southern/

border state city—an important element in the regional politics of the nation. Southern and border state Republicans have been contesting effectively in many presidential, gubernatorial, and congressional races. But in Nashville, as in many southern cities, they are poorly organized on a nuts and bolts basis at the local level. As a result, the only formal organization of consequence— and even that is often suspect—is found among the Democrats. Houston symbolizes the exploding economic and population centers of the sunbelt. Houston and cities like it, riding the crest of the demand for energy and new technology, are in a process of accelerated change. Because the population shift to the sunbelt has also shifted the balance of political power, Houston and its sister cities may well represent the politics of the future. The extent to which political parties are organized and active in Houston and other urban areas should present a rough insight into the state of the nation's local party operations.

A Social Profile of Party Activists

An examination of parties at any level normally begins with the people who staff them, the degree to which they are representative of their communities, and the extent to which their demographic characteristics provide an indication of the differing natures of the two parties and their coalitions.

Comparing the available data (Table 9.2), it appears that most party workers are long-time residents of their communities (data not shown) and that they do reflect, on some indicators, the social division of their populations. Most are men (in Chicago–Cook County virtually all are men, in contrast to the border-state city of Nashville, where less than half are men and party politics are less organized). Most are white, although Detroit Democrats more accurately reflect the racial composition of their city than do Chicago, Houston, or Nashville Democrats. Most party activists are middle aged and higher up the socioeconomic scale than the populations they represent, a common finding in studies of political representation.

As Table 9.3 shows, most party activists have been politically involved for many years (anywhere from 50 percent to 90 percent have worked in politics for ten years or more). Most party members studied had considerable contact with upper level organizational leaders, indicating a degree of cohesion within the parties not entirely expected. Also, most appear to have a voice in party 113

TABLE 9.2 ■ Social Profile of Party Workers in Five Urban Areas, 1980[a]

	Chicago			Detroit			Los Angeles			Houston			Nashville[b]
	D	R	T	D	R	T	D	R	T	D	R	T	D
Sex													
Male	97	93	94	58	62	59	63	63	63	72	65	69	44
Female	3	7	6	42	38	41	37	37	37	28	35	31	56
Age													
Under 40	80	89	84	32	35	32	36	27	–	16	20	11	–
Over 40	20	11	16	68	65	68	64	83	–	84	80	54	–
Race													
Black	10	21	16	59	35	52	–	–	–	19	5	11	28
White	90	79	84	41	65	48	–	–	–	77	95	86	72
Education													
High school or less	33	49	41	20	14	17	29	30	30	53	46	50	40
College	67	51	59	80	86	83	71	70	71	47	54	50	60
Occupation[c]													
Blue collar	–	–	–	33	39	34	–	–	–	–	–	–	–
White collar	95	91	93	50	68	56	74	85	80	58	71	62	68
Other	5	9	7	–	–	–	–	–	–	31	21	25	14
Religion[d]													
Catholic	50	48	55	32	39	34	16	19	18	30	9	20	8
Protestant	39	40	30	44	41	–	40	65	53	63	76	69	68
Jewish	11	12	13	4	5	5	19	7	12	3	0	2	12

[a] In percent. Total may not add up to 100 percent due to rounding or missing information. Column T refers to the composite for both parties. Where there is no figure, data were unavailable.
[b] The Nashville study included only Democrats.
[c] Figures represent approximations. The category "other" includes not known, retired, housewife, student, etc.
[d] Figures represent those in the sample who claimed a religion. Due to missing information, totals do not add up to 100%.

TABLE 9.3 ■ Professional Experience of Party Workers in Five Urban Areas, 1980[a]

Professional Experience	Chicago D	Chicago R	Chicago T	Detroit D	Detroit R	Detroit T	Los Angeles D	Los Angeles R	Los Angeles T	Houston D	Houston R	Houston T	Nashville D
Years active in party work													
Less than 5	7	5	5	21	42	30	–	–	–	8	9	9	24
5–10	4	2	4	17	6	15	–	–	–	11	20	15	8
11 or more	89	93	91	62	52	55	74	72	73	81	61	76	61
Interaction with other party leaders[b]													
District leaders	76	61	68	63	32	53	–	–	–	–	–	–	68
County leaders	81	69	75	31	19	27	71	68	70	–	–	–	78
State leaders	51	34	45	28	11	23	35	29	33	–	–	–	14
Strength of partisanship													
High	87	81	–	53	34	–	71	81	–	43	43	43	–
Moderate	11	14	–	41	52	–	22	15	–	39	56	49	–
Low	2	5	–	6	14	–	7	4	–	18	11	8	–

[a] In percent. Totals may not add to 100 percent due to rounding or missing information. Where there is no figure, data were unavailable.
[b] Weekly or monthly meetings.

operations and could be considered moderately strong (Houston, Detroit) to strong (Chicago, Los Angeles) party advocates. There is, however, a great deal of variance among cities on individual measures, which suggests there is a much more cohesive party structure top to bottom for the Chicago Democrats, for example, in contrast to Detroit Republicans, and that parties in some areas may not extend upwards much beyond the county level (e.g., Nashville).

Although political motivations (data not shown) vary from one urban area to another, the most consistent finding is that party activity results from ideological and community-oriented reasons. Personal reasons—either the social aspect or the desire to advance business interests—are significantly less important. Overall, it may be the degrees of difference that assume importance. For example, the commitment to party is strong in Chicago politics, as it is in most other areas. But "politics as a way of life," one of the indicators, has a different meaning and requires a greater degree of commitment for those who grew up in a machine-dominated area and who devote themselves to political work. Seventy percent of Chicago Democrats, 32 percent of suburban Cook County Democrats, and an equally impressive 70 percent of suburban Cook County Republicans have been in politics for over twenty years. Supporting, or fighting the machine and its candidates truly does become a way of life. Forty-three percent of the Chicago Democrats worked fifty hours or more a week at their jobs during elections. In truth, of course, this was their job and any other work was incidental. No other party can claim such a commitment.

Two to three times as many Chicago-area Democrats as Republicans enter politics to begin a career, make business contacts, and to be close to influential people. Republicans, or anyone in areas dominated by the other party, must content themselves with more abstract, less personalized considerations as spurs to involvement.

The extent to which local party organizations devoted their time and resources to three of the more critical aspects of electoral mobilization—registration, door-to-door canvassing, and election day get-out-the-vote drives—was impressive (Table 9.4). While again there are differences among the localities, the overall impression is that local parties are organized and active in campaigns. Judging by the limited data presented, political parties in the urban areas studied—and possibly urban areas in general, if the cities

TABLE 9.4 ■ Percent of Party Activities in Five Urban Areas, 1980[a]

Activities	Chicago			Detroit			Los Angeles			Houston			Nashville
	D	R	T	D	R	T	D	R	T	D	R	T	D
Voter registration	–	–	–	42	19	–	60	72	–	80	77	–	88
House to house canvassing	95	98	96	60	61	–	53	48	–	36	49	–	68
Election day activities	–	–	–	69	62	–	68	77	–	47	43	–	56
Hours per week spent on campaign activity													
Up to 10	2	4	3	41	53	–	43	46	–	–	–	–	32
11–19	23	14	20	19	18	–	22	20	–	–	–	–	18
20 or more	75	82	77	40	29	–	34	35	–	–	–	–	50

[a] In percent. Totals may not add to 100 percent due to rounding or missing information. Where there is no figure, data were unavailable.

examined are indicative of what is taking place nationwide—are manned by experienced and involved individuals, and are engaging in a range of electoral activities that suggest political parties at the local level, rather than being dead, are simply underappreciated.

Local Parties Over Time

Some comparisons of party personnel and activities over time are possible. For example, Samuel J. Eldersveld has been systematically examining a sample of thirty-eight precincts in Detroit at eight year intervals (1956, 1964, 1972, 1980).[11] Dwaine Marvick, in one of the rare over-time analyses of any party elite,[11] has surveyed the ideological, motivational, and demographic attributes of party activists and the activity levels of local parties in the Los Angeles area in 1963, 1968, 1972, 1976, 1978, and 1980. An examination of their data suggests that more women (although their number still isn't proportionate to their percentage of the population), more highly educated men and women, and more careerists are becoming party activists. This finding is consistent with other studies (see below). There is an increasing emphasis on more politically experienced party workers who, at the same time, are substantially less motivated by party loyalty, per se, or generalized feelings of goodwill and obligation to the community.

In Detroit, between 1956 and 1980, there appears to have been more interaction among party levels and more cohesion within the party organization. Party activists today aspire more to higher levels within the organization, a good sign for a continuing revitalization of upper-level personnel. They also are less motivated by blind loyalty and want more of a direct say in party operations and decision-making. In Los Angeles, the motivational patterns over time bear many resemblances to those in Detroit: While party loyalty and community obligation are less important, the desire to influence politics, an increasing feeling that politics is a way of life and an increasing emphasis on political careers, although the numbers claiming this to be "very important" are still small (one-fifth of the sample), have become more important as attractions to party involvement for Los Angeles cadremen. Eldersveld found that activists—whatever their reasons for joining initially—continued in politics because they liked the work and their associates and derived satisfaction from political involvement.

Political parties may be in the process of becoming more ideologically distinct. At least, among party activists over time, there is evidence of a polarization of political beliefs (Democrats more liberal, Republicans more conservative).

In relation to key activities (registration, campaign canvassing, and election day get-out-the-vote drives), the Detroit precincts demonstrate about the same levels of effort as they did a generation ago, with one exception. There has been a sharp decline in registration drives among Democrats. The reasons why are not clear. The Los Angeles party cadremen invest about the same amount of time and effort in party work as those originally sampled.

Minorities continue to be underrepresented in party positions although their share among party activists has increased. In Detroit, for example, blacks constitute 63 percent of the population (judging by national trends, they probably vote 80–90 percent Democratic) and control 59 percent of Democratic precinct positions, up from 26 percent in 1956. They control 35 percent of Republican positions, an increase of 15 percent from 1956.

A study of Pittsburgh precinctmen gives some support to these findings. The authors compared party workers in 1976 with those in 1971 and found them to be politically more experienced, slightly better educated, and to have longer tenure in their jobs. The sharpest difference was the decline in patronage appointees (especially in Democratic ranks) among activists. In most other respects—activity emphases, motivations, and personal characteristics—the two samples were similar. The time span is not great so caution may be advisable in generalizing from the findings.

Even Chicago politics have changed. In comparing the 1980 results with studies done by Harold F. Gosnell in 1928 and 1936, differences are apparent. Gosnell described the different backgrounds of the ward committeemen of this early era thusly:[12]

> Since the legal profession is very closely related to
> business, finance and commerce and since the business
> leaders tend to be Republican . . . it is natural that
> there would be more lawyers among the Republican
> than among the Democratic committeemen. Some of
> the Republican ward committeemen who are lawyers
> do not make a profession out of politics. Their main
> interest is in the law, and politics is a side line for
> them . . . a number of Democratic committeemen
> who started as clerks or saloonkeepers make politics
> their profession. Many of these men lack the

119

> necessary educational background to go into law. A
> few of the Democratic ward bosses who are lawyers
> belong to firms which are notorious for their
> connections with the big tax-dodgers and the leading
> figures of the underworld. Several ward
> committeemen were members of a law firm which
> had a large criminal practice with prominent
> gangsters as clients and also a large tax-receivership
> practice.

Judging by Table 9.2, all the outward signs are that Democratic commiteemen have changed substantially, now ranking high on the socioeconomic scale.

Two things, however, are little changed. Machine politicians still come up through the ranks. Generation after generation puts in its apprenticeship, learns the political game, and moves up gradually in power, responsibility, and material rewards. This was true of Jake Arvey in the first quarter of the century when he sponsored Adlai Stevenson, Paul Douglas, and mayor Richard J. Daley. It was true of Daley and his ally within the party, George W. Dunne, Daley's successor as head of the cook County Democratic organization. It is true of Edward Vrydolyak, once considered a "young Turk" and now Dunne's successor as Cook County party leader. It is true also of Daley's son, former ward boss and present state's attorney, Richard M. Daley.

Unchanged as well is the machine's success in electoral politics and the strength of its relationship to its supporters. Two precinct captains, one Italian and the other Polish, both in their late sixties, explained to Milton Rakove:

> Italian captain: My job [is] as a precinct captain. In the last
> twenty years, I devoted 365 days a year to politics. My
> telephone number is given to everybody in the precinct,
> and I told them, "No matter what time of the day or
> night, you call me if you need me." I never like to
> hear anybody say, "Gee, we only see you on election
> day." There are 365 days and you got 600 people in the
> precinct. . . . I have devoted many, many days to the
> precinct to be a successful precinct captain and a good
> precinct captain. You have to know your people. You
> have to be there for their wants and needs.
> Communication and service is the success of a precinct
> captain.[13]

Polish captain: The very first thing I do each morning, I get my car out of the garage and I take a ride through the alleys. Many of the people, the Latinos and some of these nonresident landlords, they have a piece of furniture to throw out in the alley, or a mattress, and I'm afraid that punks will set a match to it and set a garage fire. I make a list. I stop at the ward yard at 20th and Damen and give it to the superintendent, and ask them if they have a bulk truck, because I know garbage men don't pick them up. If not today, possibly tomorrow. And they'll pick it up. I also see when a man needs a garbage can. I have access to garbage cans in my yard [the Sanitation Department], always a dozen on hand for my precinct. If a fella really needs one, I'll tell him, "Look, when you get home from work, come over and pick one up." They're happy to get them. Also, the Latinos ask questions or explanations of some of the papers they get. Many times, if they have a traffic violation, we have a lawyer in the organization who goes and represents these lads in court for no fee to them. That's a free service that the organization provides if a fella gets a ticket. But there is no such thing, like some guys say, "Fix it!"[14]

These precinct workers could be describing the machine's relationship and the services rendered to its Irish, Italian, or German voters of four to six generations ago.

▓▓▓ CONCLUSION

It may be that political parties are alive and well in those areas that allow them to contest for elective office at the local level. It also may be that it is far too early to tell, the studies presented not withstanding. The limited evidence available is encouraging, but restricted in scope and applicability. And the fact still remains that despite obvious problems for the exercise of democratic representation, most cities are non-partisan.

CHAPTER 10

PRESIDENTIAL SELECTION: REFORM AND ITS CONSEQUENCES

■■■ THE "OLD SYSTEM"

There has been a revolution in presidential nominating methods since the late sixties. The nominating system in use for the generation prior to this emphasized closed decision-making with nominations awarded on the basis of negotiations among interest group representatives and party leaders. This meant, for example, that in the Democratic party the most formidable state and local party leaders and the top leadership of the AFL could effectively decide the nomination. Those most influential within the system were the politicians, like Mayor Richard J. Daley of Chicago or Governor David Lawrence of Pennsylvania, who could deliver all or most of their state's national convention delegate vote to the candidate they backed, and the AFL-CIO's George Meaney, a man of decided opinions on all aspects of domestic and foreign policy who spoke for organized labor and could deliver, or withhold, its endorsement. The negotiating within the Republican party, as closed as the Democratic party's processes, was basically the same. The groups represented at the power center, however (business and state party leaders), were different and the ideological split within the party (between the right wing, the

Taft-Goldwater-Nixon branch, and the moderate/centrists, the Rockefeller-Scranton-Eisenhower wing) were, if anything, more severe than the factional splits in the Democratic party.

Within this "old party system," grass-roots party members and the public had little say. Primary elections were taken as "advisory," demonstrating specific features of a candidate's campaign (the ability to win in a "hostile" state; an appeal to a voting bloc thought to be antagonistic; a demonstration of a mastery of campaigning; greater popular appeal). It would seem that such a system was unaccountable and unresponsive, or at best indirectly responsive, to a party's constituency and that it would be only a matter of time before serious problems developed. This is exactly what happened.

◼◼◼ A TIME OF CHANGE

The mid- to late sixties proved to be a period of enormous social disruption. The discontent fed student protests, public marches, an unrelentingly strident rhetoric, and the rise of innumerable protest and extremist groups. The crises centered on the government's role in pursuing the Vietnam War and, not incidentally, the domestic and personal costs of those policy decisions. The frustration boiled over into demonstrations of various sorts and into repeated acts of violence. Police and student/demonstrator confrontations became commonplace. The government seemed cut-off, unable or unwilling to respond effectively to the discontent that engulfed the country. The consequence was an authority crisis that divided the nation.

With each new confrontation came an appeal to "work within the system." In the 1968 election year, many of the antiwar protestors decided to do just that. They focused on the Democratic party, the party in power and the one that had unremittingly pursued the war. First they banded together behind Eugene McCarthy and, until his assassination, Robert Kennedy, in an effort to win the Democratic party's presidential nomination and/or change the course of its policy. While their candidates did well in the popular vote, they won relatively few national convention seats. The nominating system proved to be more arbitrary and unresponsive than anyone had imagined. For example, when President Lyndon Johnson withdrew from the race after the New Hampshire primary, early polls indicating a lack of public support, Vice President Hu-   123 bert Humphrey became the heir apparent. Humphrey did not formally contest any primaries prior to the national convention, yet he won the party's nomination overwhelmingly. But at a price. The convention itself, held in Chicago, turned out to be the most violent in either party's history. Humphrey went on to lose a close race to Richard M. Nixon.

■■■■ REFORM AND THE PARTIES

In the wake of the national convention, party regulars and reformers determined that nothing of this sort should ever occur again. Out of this decision came the reform movement.[1]

Both parties have had a number of reform commissions, the Democrats continuing the process to the present day (Table 10.1), but it is not necessary to review the contributions of each of them.[2] Basically, the Democrats were concerned with renovating presidential selection practices, opening them, and making them more representative of the rank and file party membership; modernizing national convention procedures; and restructuring the national party's organization. The procedures of the national convention were made more efficient, although the convention itself was little changed. The introduction of the party charter and midterm policy conferences, both products of the reform period, have had an effect on the national party but to date it has been limited.[3] The broader goal of molding a more effective and responsive national party has not been achieved.

The Republican reform commissions proposed a number of modest changes in party operations but they have had little impact for several reasons. First, the Republicans have always been a much better organized party than the Democrats. The potential for substantial change in this regard was limited. The emphasis thus became one of finding more effective means to achieve established goals, rather than to restructure and redirect the party apparatus. Second, the Republicans have a much smaller coalition, more demographically and politically homogenous, which has been satisfied with its party's elaborate procedures, the candidates nominated, and the policy commitments made. If anything, the Republican party was suspicious of reform. Consequently, the major changes took place within the Democratic party in relation to presidential selection. As it turned out, these were monumental.

TABLE 10.1 ■ Reform Commissions, by Party and Area of Interest

Democratic Party		
Presidential Nominations	National Convention Modernization	Reform Party Structure
McGovern-Fraser Commission (1968–1972)	O'Hare Commission (1968–1972)	Sanford Commission (1972–1974)
Mikulski Commission (1972–1974)		
Compliance Review Commission (1974–1976)		
Winograd Commission (1975–1976 1976–1978)		
Compliance Review Commission (1978–1980)		
Hunt Commission (1980–1982)	Platform Accountability Commission (1980–1984)	

Republican Party
National Convention Improvement and Recommendations to States on Delegate Selection
DO (Delegates and Organizations) Committee (1968–1972)
Rule 29 Committee (1972–1974)

■ REFORMING PRESIDENTIAL SELECTION

The reform movement encouraged greater participation in presidential selection within the political parties; tried to establish fair procedures for presidential selection; and tried to switch control over presidential nominations from a small elite acting in the name of the party to the grass-roots membership, exemplified by those participating in the prenomination phase of selection.[4] Suceeding on all counts, the movement constituted a revolution in presidential selection: Ultimate power moved from a handful of political figures ruling over a seemingly closed system and transferred 125

TABLE 10.2 ■ The Growth of Primaries in Presidential Nominations

Year	Democrat (%)	Republican (%)
1968	17	16
1972	23	22
1976	30	29
1980	33	34

Source: Democratic and Republican National Conventions.

to institutions open to all party members who wished to participate. The reform movement changes were bitterly resisted and continue to be a matter of public debate.[5] The reform efforts within the Democratic party have been reassessed by a number of party committees, most of which attempted, in varying degrees, to close the procedures established during the first wave of reforms. The counter-movement has continued into the eighties.[6]

■■■ THE IMPACT OF THE REFORMS

A number of changes have taken place in presidential selection since the beginning of the reform period in the late sixties. Foremost has been the increase in the number and importance of primaries (Table 10.2).[7] The Democrats held seventeen primaries in 1968 and thirty-three in 1980, the Republicans sixteen in 1968 and thirty-four in 1980. In 1984, there has been a drop of approximately five primaries in each party, but they remain the dominant means of selection national convention delegates. Approximately one-third of the delegates to the 1968 convention were selected through primaries. Because many of these delegates were uncommitted (Illinois, Pennsylvania, Ohio, and other major urban states), they simply followed the lead of the party bosses who then controlled the system. Today, roughly 75 percent of the delegates from both parties are chosen through primaries and are committed to the presidential candidate under whose banner they ran and for whom party voters indicated support. In fact, it had been feared that primary elections would completely replace the state party convention and caucus process. For better or worse, primaries now play a far more significant role in presidential nomination than ever before.

TABLE 10.3 ■ Minority Group Influence Within the Parties

National Convention	Blacks (%)	Women (%)	Youth (under 30) (%)
	Democrats		
1968	7	13	4
1972	15	40	22
1976	11	33	15
1980	14	49	11
	Republicans		
1968	2	17	1
1972	3	35	7
1976	3	31	7
1980	3	29	—

Source: Democratic and Republican National Committees.

Along with the rise in the influence of primaries, minority group representation within the system and specifically within the Democratic party increased (Table 10.3). This was one of the objectives of the reform movement and it appears to have borne fruit,[8] witness the gains by women in both parties, the mounting influence of blacks at Democratic party conventions, and the increased involvement of young people (of the groups examined, though, this is the least cohesive and politically significant). Along with increased minority group representation and the spread of primaries, there has been dramatic increase in the number of people participating in the nominating system (Table 10.4). From 1968 to 1980, participation increased almost threefold in both parties and in caucus/convention and primary systems.

A major goal of the reforms was to allow more people to participate. From 1968 to 1972 participation jumped 10 million and has been increasing ever since.

The differences between the old party system and the new one are substantial. Because as people in general are participating more, the role of professional politicians in the process—at least in the Democratic party—appears to be on the decline. Democratic United States Senators and Congressmen represented 14 percent of the membership of the national convention in 1980, down from an average of 75 percent and 41 percent, respectively, in pre-re-

TABLE 10.4 ■ Participation in Prenomination Presidential Selection

Year	Democrats			Republicans		
	Primary	Caucus	Total	Primary	Caucus	Total
1968	(17) 8,247,000	(34) 219,000	8.4 million	(16) 4,571,000	(35) 105,000	4.7 million
1972	(23) 16,715,000	(28) 771,000	17.5 million	(22) 5,887,000	(29) 256,000	6.1 million
1976	(31) 18,884,000	(20) 639,000	19.5 million	(30) 9,724,000	(21) 546,000	10.3 million
1980	(33) 17,580,000	(18) 539,000	18.1 million	(35) 13,301,000	(16) 370,000	13.7 million

Grand Total Particpating

1968	13.1 million
1972	23.6 million
1976	29.8 million
1980	31.8 million

Source: Democratic and Republican National Committees.

TABLE 10.5 ■ Elective Officeholders as Delegates to Democratic National Conventions

	Old Party System (1956–1968)	New Party System (1972–1976)	1980 National Convention
Percent of Democratic senators	75	27	14
Percent of U.S. representatives	41	15	14
Percent of governors	82	64	74

Source: Democratic National Committee.

form days (Table 10.5). Governors have done better, although their number and proportionate influence have declined also.

To deal with this problem, the Democrats directed that an extra 10 percent (in 1980) to 25 percent or more (in 1984) be added to each state's national convention delegation and that these extra delegates be reserved for party professionals. The idea, orginally, was that these professionals would bring experience and judgment to national convention deliberations; that they would be unswayed by the passions and candidates of the moment; and that they would add a corrective balance to the decisions made by the grass-roots activists. Judging by the 1980 convention, at least, this has not happened: The "add-on" delegates turned out to be as committed to their candidates as the activists who voted in the primary. The new delegates apparently exercised no more independent judgment while at the convention than did the activists.

The new party system has witnessed a collapse in party control over its own nominating process. Beyond specifying the rules, the parties today exert little control over individual campaigns since candidates have their own organizations and are subsidized by federal funds.

The new power center is the media, especially television. Candidates pay for air time exposure. Success is perceived as winning in Iowa or New Hampshire. It brings money, volunteers, a better standing at the polls, and a *Newsweek* or *Time* cover (George Bush in 1980, Gary Hart in 1984). Once this has happened, a candidate has become a serious contender. The media determines this; throughout the primaries they define the winners and losers. The delegate count follows the media success of the candidate. Television has become the most powerful instrument in the prenomination phase and probably in the post-nomination phase as 129 well. The role of television in the electoral process has become a subject of concern.

Along with the shift in the role of the parties, the decline in their power over nominations, and the rise in significance of the media, there has been a change in the status of the national convention. Under the old party system, the national convention was the single most important occurrence in the nominating struggle and in the life and management of a political party. Today national conventions merely ratify decisions made in the state primaries and caucuses. The most important function of national conventions has been usurped collectively by the state parties. However, they are still important in framing a platform (as the Democrats showed in 1980); determining the rules for party management in the period between elections; choosing an acceptable vice presidential candidate (as the Republicans showed in 1980 and the Democrats in 1984); unifying the party (as both 1984 national conventions demonstrated); and launching the fall general election campaign. Is this enough? Probably not. It is unlikely that television will continue to cover national conventions, gavel to gavel, as they have in the past, thus the importance of the national convention is likely to continue its decline.

Finally, the nominating process itself is getting longer and longer, candidates declaring earlier and earlier. The 1980 campaign can serve as an example. Once elected president Jimmy Carter never stopped running for renomination. In 1977 he began setting in place the nominating rules for 1980. Then, a year before the first primaries, he began building his state organizations, periodically visiting the states himself (especially New Hampshire and Iowa), or sending his family, campaign officials, and members of his administration. His "town meetings" and media consultants kept his name constantly before the public.

It is also fair to say that Ronald Reagan never stopped running. After losing a close race to Gerald Ford in 1976, Reagan kept himself in the public eye through a syndicated radio show and a syndicated newspaper column. He used his excess campaign funds to start a personal PAC to fund conservative candidates and causes. His organization was in place a year before the convention and he began his active campaign with the announcement of his candidacy in November of 1979. The less visible candidates declare as early or even earlier. Congressman Philip Crane, who sought the Republican party's nomination, announced on August 2, 1978, twenty-seven months before the 1980 general election. He campaigned in forty-four states, gave 2,500 speeches, and spent $5 million. His results were a debt of $200,000, three national convention delegates, and potentially libelous personal attacks in two publications.

In the spring and early summer of 1979, the 1980 Kennedy campaign began with the formation of draft-Kennedy committees in twenty-six states. Also by early summer a national draft-Kennedy organization had been created to complement the state units. The ADA endorsed Kennedy for President in June of 1979, and liberal and conservative senators and congressmen (Henry Jackson and George McGovern, for example) urged him, publicly and privately, to run for the good of the party. Pressure was placed on Kennedy to indicate his intentions by Labor Day. He announced in early September that his family no longer objected to his candidacy and that he would actively consider running. This was taken by his supporters as tantamount to an announcement of candidacy, which it was. On November 7, Kennedy made his formal announcement.

It is noteworthy that the first contest between Kennedy and Carter took place in Florida in the fall of 1979, before the election year had even begun. No delegates were at stake—it was purely a media event—but it was considered important to demonstrate the relative strength of the two candidates. The Carter Administration poured people, money, federal jobs, and appointments into the state. They out-organized and out-maneuvered the Kennedy camp, winning a nonbinding straw poll at the state convention, which was duly reported by the media. The event was significant because it re-emphasized the fact that Carter was a fierce campaigner and that he knew how to use the powers of incumbency. It also served as a preview of what was to come—the Kennedy forces never got organized, never settled on a theme for the campaign, and never effectively challenged the president. Not only did the fight begin early, but it ended early as well since Carter's victories in Iowa and New Hampshire effectively eliminated Kennedy from the race. Although Kennedy played out the string, only a drastic turn of events would have won him the nomination. The race was over, for all practical purposes, by February.

At the beginning of the Republican party's prenomination battle, George Bush won a close vote in Iowa. By New Hampshire, Reagan had corrected his campaign problems and won convincingly. From then on, Reagan, like Carter, won one major   131 victory after another. There were occasional lapses in both campaigns, but nothing of consequence (a "dip in the road" as Carter's campaign manager would call them). The delegates piled up for both men. The only interest aroused by the Republican campaign was the timing of withdrawal announcements by the other contenders: Senator Robert Dole dropped out in February; Senator Howard Baker days before the Illinois primary in March; former Nixon cabinet secretary John Connally in March after his failure in the South Carolina primary; Crane in March; Congressman John Anderson in late April to form an independent party candidacy; and Bush, the last of the challengers, in late May. The nomination races were effectively over in late February. One reason the races seem so long is that they formally begin as early as two to four years before the first delegates are chosen. For example, former Vice President Walter Mondale effectively began campaigning for the 1984 Democratic nomination in 1981, and by 1982 undeclared candidates John Glenn, Gary Hart, Alan Cranston, Reuben Askew, and Kennedy were all "testing the waters."

In turn, the prenomination race can end, for all practical purposes, in late winter of the election year. Yet the primaries, caucuses, and media attention continue through the long spring and summer. As a consequence, the process appears to go on forever.

Finally, because of the frequent redefinition of rules and procedures, the presidential nominating system seems to be ever-changing and difficult to master or understand. This constant effort to modify the system has resulted as much from the quadrennial desire to reshape nominating methods to better represent a prospective candidate's or party faction's best interests as it has from attempts to correct deficiencies in the operations of the process. Not surprisingly, the presidential election procedures that result have come under sustained attack.

■■■■ RESTRUCTURING PRESIDENTIAL NOMINATIONS—AGAIN[9]

Morris Udall has argued that "the current system of choosing our [presidential] nominees is too long, too difficult, too expensive. It emphasizes the wrong kinds of skills and encourages the wrong kinds of society."[10] Udall is not alone in his indictment of presidential selection methods. The Duke University Forum on Presidential Nominations in its evaluation of the presidential

nomination process opined that

. . . the present system ill serves the purposes of the nation. It saps interest, distorts choice, eliminates judgment, narrows the popular base, spans too long a period, and squeezes out of the deliberative process those peers whose evaluations and cooperation the choice of a President vitally requires. Most significantly, the present system radically erodes the foundations of the one institution most necessary to its effective operation: the political party.[11]

The condemnation of present methods appears to be universal. Not surprisingly, a number of proposals—some quite radical—have been advanced to remedy present deficiencies and somehow procure the kind of enlightened and humane leadership needed to guide the country through its continuing crises.

The Reform Proposals

Among the proposals being put forward are the following:

Concerning Presidential Nominations Generally

- Restrict the delegate selection to a four (or five, or three) month period.

- Funnel most (or all) funds for pre-nomination campaigns through the national committees (rather than from the Federal Election Commission directly to the candidates who qualify).

- Create a national commission through congressional legislation to coordinate and simplify state delegate selection rules and practices and to ensure broadly comparable systems in each of the states.

- Allow all party members to participate in presidential delegate selection.

- Require nondiscriminatory affirmative action guarantees for all delegate selection procedures.

- Require, through party-mandated rules, a proper mix of primary and caucus delegate selection systems by the states to ensure that no one system dominates (this is usually directed against primaries).

- Limit the role of the media in the process and their effect on the final outcome (both within states and nationally). Although this has been discussed extensively, no reasonable or legal means have been put forward to accomplish such an end.

- Require state and national parties to adopt explicit rules, available to party members and the media, governing all aspects of delegate selection and presidential nominations. (This has been largely accomplished, although critics have questioned the lack of specificity in some rules and an inadequate pre-convention appeals or adjudication process in the event of controversy.)

- Restrict the role of the grassroots party membership in the process.

- Ban formal delegate commitments to presidential candidates in a move to introduce more flexibility into national convention procedures.

- Increase (from recent 10 percent to 15 percent levels) the proportionate share of the vote needed by presidential contenders before they can claim any national convention delegate votes from a given state. In some proposals, it is argued that the "winner-take-all" principle be reinstituted at the state level. The belief is that such requirements favor centrists and the best-known presidential contenders (including incumbents) and work against factional candidates and outsiders.

Concerning Primaries

- Institute a national primary to select all national convention delegates.

- Combine a national primary that would select a specified proportion of the national convention delegates (normally two-thirds) with a mechanism through which the state and national parties would appoint the remaining delegates from party and elective officeholders.

- Abolish all state primaries.

- Make the state primaries advisory only in the delegate selection process.

- Introduce regional primaries through congressional legislation (the most common assumption) or party mandate. Depending on the plan, the country would be divided into four of five regions with primaries held in each region at three to four week intervals. The regional ordering (first, second, etc.) would be decided by lot or held on a rotation basis. States would be free to hold, or not hold, a primary, but only on the date specified for the region.

- Adopt "approval voting" in primaries. Developed by Steven J. Brams, this system permits primary voters to vote for any of the presidential contenders on the primary ballot they favor. The result is a heavier vote for centrists and candidates with broad support across the party spectrum, and a weaker cumulative vote for fringe and lesser-known candidates, who presumably have the advantage under present one-candidate vote limitations.

Concerning Party Caucuses

- Return to a dominant caucus system in delegate selection.

- Require that *all* delegate selection be through caucuses or some combination of the caucus/convention system at the state and local levels.

- Require due process and fair procedure rules to ensure open and representative caucus proceedings.

- Schedule all party caucuses on uniform dates within a state (or region) to maximize public knowledge and media coverage of the meetings and their deliberations.

- Randomly select caucus participants by lot to represent the local party at the next highest level of delegate selection (county, state, or national convention). This method is intended to ensure an accurate reflection of the concerns of the party base in higher-level presidential selection deliberation (used by Florida Republicans in 1979).

Concerning National Conventions

- Reduce the size of the national convention to make it a more deliberative body.

- Hold national conventions earlier in the election year (May or June).

135

■■■■ SOME OBSERVATIONS ON THE CONTINUING REFORM OF THE PRESIDENTIAL NOMINATING SYSTEM—A WORD IN FAVOR OF DISCRETION

Some of the proposed changes, e.g., the national primary, would introduce radical transformations into presidential politics. Others, seemingly more innocuous, would result in profound (although all the implications are not clear and cannot be foreseen) and more than likely unwelcome consequences for the political parties and for presidential nominations. For example, proposals for a national commission to standardize quialifications for state delegation selection and for regional primaries or caucus dates would require congressional action. Such proposals would introduce a federal presence into an area that has remained remarkably free of such an influence. It is not unreasonable, then, to believe that at some time rules will be adopted that favor a congressional influence or the interests of national party leaders or national-level interests groups. If so, the state parties and their rank and file would probably suffer a diminishing influence over the entire process. A federal presence in the system might well result in procedures that are too unyielding to subtle shifts in power and the needs of the state and national parties, which would not be an asset to a party system struggling to expand its base and prove its relevance in a time of dramatic social and technological change.

Presidential selection is unlikely to return to the old pre-reform system since it failed to adapt adequately to a changing society. The Duke University Commission report made the point well:

> [The] . . . goal of strengthening the role of the national convention [and modifying the nominating system] should not be interpreted as a call for a "return" to a supposed golden age when cigar-smoking party bosses ran state delegations like their own political fiefdoms. Mainly beneficial changes over the past few decades have made this kind of a desire for [a] return to the good old days a re-election of misplaced nostalgia rather than a realistic proposal.[12]

One final note on the continuing changes in the nominating process: In all the various remappings of the presidential selection

TABLE 10.6 ■ Public Satisfaction with Political and Social Institutions

Topic and Percent Agreeing
75% are satified with primaries
70% think the nominating system is basically sound
62% think the political system is basically sound
53% are satisfied with political parties
10% think party leaders and officeholders should have more influence than they do now
7% respect public officeholders

Source: *Los Angeles Times* survey of December, 1979.

procedures, the public was never asked what it thought. This oversight isn't unusual since political parties often respond to internally-generated, short-run forces relatively isolated from the broader political world. Much of later reform efforts operated in such an atmosphere. The accomodations introduced were intended primarily to meet the needs of elective officeholders and party professionals: Grass-roots or broader public concerns were of secondary importance.

Aware of the absence of any reliable data on public attitudes toward nominating processes, the *Los Angeles Times* undertook a survey to assess the electorate's view of presidential selection forms. The results were surprising. Eight out of ten voters were satisfied with the primaries—a target of many of the later changes in selection procedures—and seven out of ten believed the nominating system to be basically sound (Table 10.6). Even more unexpected was the strength of support given present nominating procedures, which were viewed more positively than the private enterprise system, political decision-making structures more generally, or the judicial process (Table 10.7). Only one in ten respondents thought that party leaders and officeholders should have more influence in the system, a change strongly supported by most party professionals. The principal findings were unequivocal: Americans are much more satisfied with the way they choose presidential nominees than with the political system as a whole, and the people who consider the nominating system "essentially good" outnumber those who would say the same of our capitalistic system of business and industry.[13] There appears to be little mandate for change in these figures.

TABLE 10.7 ■ Public Perceptions of Soundness of System

	Is Basically Sound		Is Not Too Sound and Needs	
	And Essentially Good	But Needs Improve-ment	Many Improve-ments	Fundamental Overhaul
System of nominating a president	43	27	11	16
System of business and industry	30	40	15	8
Political system	17	45	19	16
System of administering justice	13	36	26	22

Source: *Los Angeles Times* survey of December, 1979.

■ CONCLUSION

Whatever the system that results from the on-going struggle over presidential selection forms, it should be left in place—with perhaps minor fine tuning—for a series of elections. An unfortunate legacy of the years since 1968 has been the constant change in rules and structures, a process that shows no evidence of abating. The present system, whatever its merits, is extraordinarily complex. The presidential nominating system should maximize the values of clarity, simplicity, and legitimacy. It should be one that best serves the parties' constituencies, and the nation. Exactly what type of system can realize these goals is the subject of intense debate. At present, the basic disagreement seems to be over how open—or closed—the system should be. The issue is yet to be decided.

CHAPTER 11

MEDIA POLITICS

■

The control political parties exercise over campaigns has lessened in recent elections, a result of the escalating costs of politics, the constant search by candidates for new sources of funds to conduct campaigns, and the increasing role of the media, especially television, in replacing the parties as the most significant channel of communication between the candidate and the voter.

■ THE PERVASIVENESS OF TELEVISION

The media have replaced political parties as the principal communicator of political news and campaign events; some would claim, although it is certainly more arguable, that they are the principal influence acting on the individual to shape his perception of, and reaction to, candidates and elections. The media, many would argue, are the major influence on presidential nominations and the outcome of elections.[1]

It is hard, if not impossible, to prove the existence of any such relationship between media influence and election results. It is clear, nonetheless, that the media have an enormous impact on American politics and that this influence has grown significantly in recent years. The media, especially television, have simply reshaped the exercise of politics in the United States. With the wan-   139 ing of party influence and an increasing independence among voters, the media have replaced the parties as the individual's principal connection with the political arena. Its influence cannot be doubted, and its limits are yet to be established.

The importance of the media (television in particular) is the direct result of technological advances and the enormous growth and mobility of the American population. Since its introduction as a serious political weapon in the presidential campaign of 1952, television has come to dominate the political scene. (Ninety-seven percent of American homes have television sets, most have more than one, and the average American spends six hours a day in front of his set. There are more televisions in the United States than telephones, cars, or bathtubs.) Today the mark of a successful campaign is television coverage, and the value of a political consultant is weighted by his ability to mold a candidate and a campaign to the peculiar needs of television. To those who succeed in this endeavor, the payoffs are enormous.

People depend on the media for their political information. Since 1960, television has been the principal source of political news for almost 90 percent of the population (Table 11.1) Newspapers provide between 50 and 80 percent of the electorate with political information (depending on the election year), while magazines and radio in recent years have declined significantly as information sources. About three out of four voters employ several media sources, but when asked what they considered the most important of these, the majority responded television, the most powerful and most personal of the outlets. No other media source approaches the status of television, a medium that (with the possible exception of radio) demands the least of its adherents. The dominance of television was established by 1956, and since 1960 two-thirds of the electorate have ranked it the most important media influences during elections.

◼◼◼ LIVING THE MEDIA LIFE

Unfortunately, and not surprisingly, there are definite patterns evident in the reliance on media. This is made clear by an examination of the number of media sources used by different social and political groups during the 1968–1976 election years (Table 11.2), a period of instability and change of direct relevance to the contemporary political scene. The table measures those employing

TABLE 11.1 ■ Percent of Media Usage, 1952–1980

Media Outlets Used by Respondents								
Outlets	1952	1956	1960	1964	1968	1972	1976	1980
Newspapers	79	68	80	78	75	57	73	73
Radio	70	45	42	49	41	43	45	50
Magazines	40	31	41	39	36	33	48	38
Television	51	74	87	89	89	88	89	87
Number of Media Outlets Used by Respondents								
Outlets	1952	1956	1960	1964	1968	1972	1976	1980
None	6	8	5	3	4	5	5	6
One	14	19	13	12	15	21	15	16
Two	30	32	28	30	32	33	23	30
Three	35	28	35	36	34	27	34	32
Four	15	13	19	19	14	13	23	16
Total	100	100	100	100	99	99	100	100

Most Important Source of Information: Selected Years				
Sources	1952	1960	1968	1980
Newspapers	26	24	24	20
Radio	32	6	4	10
Television	36	65	66	66
Magazines	6	5	6	4
Total	100	100	100	100

Source: Center for Political Studies.

a maximum of four sources—television, newspapers, radio, and magazines—minus those depending on a single source or those not using the media at all. In demographic terms, exposure to a variety of media sources is most limited among those with the least formal education, those living in rural areas, those with the lowest incomes and lowest occupational achievements, and southerners. Politically, Democrats, Independents, and the ideologically uncommitted have a limited exposure to media sources.

Another way to examine the structure of bias in media resources is to employ the same measure to investigate the number of media outlets used by people with different attitudinal orientations to elections (Table 11.3). Those with the least interest in election outcomes, the least concern over on-going campaigns or

TABLE 11.2 ■ Differentials in the Patterns of Media Use by Social and Political Groups in Selected Years, 1968–1976[a]

Social and Political Groups	1968	1972	1976
Social Groups			
1943 or later cohort	−8	−20	0
1927–1942 cohort	−3	−15	12
1911–1926 cohort	0	−7	3
1895–1910 cohort	−12	−10	−3
Before 1895 cohort	−10	−18	−13
Grade school	−24	−31	−30
High School	−9	−20	−7
College	19	8	31
Central cities	1	−5	10
Suburbs	−5	−8	7
Nonurban areas	−8	−22	−6
Income percentile 0–16	−22	−30	−30
Income percentile 17–33	−11	−19	−6
Income percentile 34–67	−3	−13	5
Income percentile 68–95	7	−5	15
Income percentile 95–100	11	14	44
Males	0	−8	14
Females	−9	−18	−5
Whites	−5	−14	5
Blacks	−4	−13	−16
Union household	−6	−19	2
Non-union household	−4	−11	4
South	−10	−17	−4
Non-south	−3	−12	6
Professional	13	12	31
White collar	−2	−7	12
Blue collar	−14	−24	−5
Unskilled	5	−13	−28
Farmers	−11	−16	−22
Housewives	−7	−26	−12
Protestants	−5	−13	1
Catholics	−5	−18	3
Jews	9	26	42
Other and no religion	−4	−13	5
Total population	−5	−14	3
Political Groups[a]			
Strong Democrats	−3	−4	11
Weak and leaning Democrats	−9	−17	1
Independent Independents	−13	−25	−4
Weak and leaning Republicans	1	−14	3
Strong Republicans	9	4	19
Liberal self placement 1	−	11	22
Liberal self placement 2	−	4	20
Neutral self placement 3	−	−17	7
Conservative self placement 4	−	−1	26

continued

TABLE 11.2 ■ Continued

Social and Political Groups	1968	1972	1976
Conservative self placement 5	–	– 2	18
Liberal index 1	4	0	9
Liberal index 2	10	1	16
Neutral index 3	– 15	– 18	– 2
Conservative index 4	– 3	– 7	16
Conservative index 5	16	– 3	30
Total population	– 5	– 14	3

Source: Center for Political Studies, as reported in Warren E. Miller, Arthur H. Miller, and Edward J. Schneider, *American National Election Studies Data Sourcebook*, Cambridge, Mass.: Harvard University Press, 1980.
[a] Figures given are the proportion of respondents who used four media sources (television, newspapers, radio, and magazines) for campaign and political information minus those using only one or none.

who wins them, little trust in others, and who feel the most alienated by government are the ones with little access to a variety of media influences. It is a good bet that to the extent that those groups are influenced by the media it is television to which they turn. This may not be all to the good since television presents the least intellectually demanding and most entertainment-oriented approach to news of all the media.

■■■■ TELEVISION, SHOW BIZ, AND CORPORATE PROFITS

Political information is available on television primarily in two forms: news programs and political commercials. News programs often tend to be bland uncontroversial. Television stations and network news programs go to extremes not to offend and thus alienate large segments of their viewing public. This means watered-down reports presented in thirty to ninety second segments, during which reporters are expected to capture the essence and significance of a story and transmit this to the viewers. They, and those anchoring the news program, attempt to do this while simultaneously presenting visuals that will excite and entertain the audience. The consequence is that the news reported is subject to an implicit bias dictated by the nature of the medium.

Given the needs of the media, it is not surprising that certain types of news events receive greater emphasis than others. The media, of course, serve a gatekeeper function: some stories are reported, others are not, some points are emphasized, others ig- 143

TABLE 11.3 ■ Differentials in the Patterns of Media Use by Political Attitudes in Selected Years, 1968–1976[a]

	1968	1972	1976	
Interest level	−49	−68	−65	Hardly
	−17	−33	−26	Only now
	1	−12	8	Some
	21	10	35	Most
Interest in campaign	−40	−43	−43	Not much
	−9	−14	3	Somewhat
	16	12	27	Very
Care who wins	−14	−32	−9	Don't care or know
	−1	−3	12	Care
President race close	−2	−9	−8	Not close
	2	−16	8	Close
Trust in gov't	−4	−17	1	Cynical
	2	−11	7	
	−6	−9	8	Trusting
Internal efficacy	−22	−26	−22	Least efficacious
	−5	−23	3	
	4	−2	19	
	18	9	34	Most efficacious
External efficacy	−16	−24	−8	Least efficacious
	−2	−9	7	
	−3	−4	20	
	8	−5	20	Most efficacious
Gov't responsiveness	−26	−25	−21	Low
	−10	−21	1	
	−8	−19	3	
	4	−6	11	
	8	−2	24	Highest
Approve of protest	−5	−17	–	Disapproval
	−2	−15	–	
	−3	−14	–	
	4	−7	–	
	11	−4	–	Approval
Citizen duty	–	−32	−30	Lowest
	–	−15	5	
	–	−8	13	Highest
Trust in people	−23	−26	−14	Least
	−6	−15	0	
	−2	−5	8	
	5	−6	17	Most
Total population	−5	−14	3	

Source: Center for Political Studies, as reported in Warren E. Miller, Arthur H. Miller, and Edward J. Schneider, *American National Election Studies Data Sourcebook*, Cambridge, Mass.: Harvard University Press, 1980.
[a] Figures given are the proportion of respondents who used four media sources (television, newspapers, radio, magazines) for campaign and political information minus those using only one or none.

nored. Selection and then condensation for presentation to a broad audience is implicit in the function of communications. Herbert J. Gans, who has studied the process, reports that many key policy and even individual story decisions are made by corporate and news executives removed from the actual reporting and news-gathering. Gans found that these executives affect the presentation of news in four ways:[2]

1. They control the budget and decisions in major personnel, thus directly and indirectly determining the adequacy, comprehensiveness, and competence of the news reporting.

2. They must protect the commercial and political interests of the firm, which is, of course, a for-profit organization. The ethics of the trade also presume that they will intervene on behalf of journalistic integrity to protect reporters from corporate management or political pressure.

3. They make the policy decisions. They decide what news is broadcast, how and when it is presented, and the manner in which sensitive issues are handled.

4. They keep abreast of daily and weekly news story selection, although normally the chief responsibility for these rests with the assignment editors and, for television, producers of the news program.

The media have varied needs. As a consequence, there is a different emphasis among them on what is reported and how it is reported. For example, it has been argued that media coverage emphasizes the personality traits of politicians and the more superficial aspects of campaigns and policy-making. Doris A. Graber has intensively analyzed the media's presentation of political news in campaigns from 1968 to 1980. The results of her study lend support to these assertions (Table 11.4). In three of the four presidential election years, the most commonly emphasized aspect of the election in newspapers was campaign events.[3] The one exception was 1968 when the turmoil over Vietnam overrode campaign considerations and set the climate in which the campaign was conducted and the electoral decision made. In the three other election years, domestic politics came in second, followed by foreign affairs, economic concerns and social issues. If anything, the pattern may even be more pronounced for television. Sixty percent of the television coverage was based on the easily photographed campaign events. Specific issue concerns were relatively neglected. 145

TABLE 11.4 ■ Emphases in the Media's Campaign Coverage of Election, 1968–1980[a]

Media Emphasis	1968	1972	1976	1980
Campaign events	14	42	51	52
Domestic politics	21	24	19	29
Foreign affairs	30	18	14	5
Economic policy	13	10	11	7
Social problems	22	7	5	6

Source: Doris Graber, "Hoopla and Horse-Race in the 1980 Campaign Coverage: A Closer Look," a paper prepared for delivery at the Annual Meeting of the Midwest Association for Public Opinion Research, 1982, November 19–20, Chicago.
[a] In percent. Percentages are based on the following number of issues: 1968: 3538; 1972: 11,187; 1976: 11,027; 1980: 147. The 1980 data come only from *The New York Times*. Data for the earlier elections come from twenty newspapers. Since news distribution patterns are quite similar among all papers, the data for a single paper are representative.

In a way, this is curious. Economic policies relevant to inflation, unemployment, and a decreasing standard of living have been major issues in recent election years and these concerns affect all voters. Why were they not better covered? Graber addresses the point: "Coverage of economic news, like unemployment, inflation, and taxes, is . . . limited because these issues are hard to explain and dramatize and rarely produce exciting pictures. Skimpy coverage may seem puzzling because these are issues with which the average voter is intimately concerned. The explanation is that most people, though concerned, are unwilling to wrestle with a difficult subject that newspeople have not yet learned to simplify and dramatize. Rather than risk writing complex campaign stories that most of the audience would probably ignore, newspeople prefer to feature the horse-race glamour of campaign events."[4]

Hence the emphasis on the seemingly less significant but safe stories concerning what the candidates did or said and their views on what the government is, or should be, doing. These two categories alone (what Graber refers to as "campaign events" and "domestic politics") accounted for almost three out of four stories reported by newspapers and television during presidential campaigns in the period 1972–1980.

Needless to say, candidates are well aware of these facts of media life and tailor their campaign accordingly. Consultants are hired to brief them on how to appear active and decisive and to schedule tours to visually graphic areas (Watts, Appalachia, supermarkets) that will stimulate good coverage. News conferences are held no later than early afternoon in order to be edited and available for the all-important early evening news programs. Candidates are drilled in how to say a few catchy words on various issues, statements that allow news editors to package them in the thirty to ninety seconds allocated for the average television news report. Candidates also go to extremes to attract a few votes, draw some free media attention, or provide footage for the evening news.[5] Average American families, are visited in their homes; appearances are made with anyone from Reggie Jackson to the Beach Boys; visits are made to nuclear plants, unemployment offices, Indian reservations, automobile factories, veterans groups.

Television is more of a mass communicator than the other media. Radio stations program for specific audiences. Those who read and/or subscribe to magazines and newspapers also represent a distinct and more limited audience. Television reports tend to be more general and less demanding of the viewer. There is a conscious effort to entertain, to avoid the "talking heads" approach of an announcer speaking directly to an audience without pictures to divert the audience, and to intersperse more serious reports with lighthearted and uplifting looks at animals, human interest features, consumer tips, weather and sports reports.

Television hosts are often chosen, as are many television reporters, for their telegenic looks rather than for their qualities as a journalist or for any particular expertise they might have in a policy area. Not surprisingly, television news personalities are considered big-time entertainers by their stations and celebrities by the public, a trend that gives some evidence of carrying over into newspaper reporting. An attractive news anchor can command big money. Barbara Walters, for example, jumped from NBC to ABC in 1976 for the then unheard of sum of $5,000,000, plus various contractual guarantees concerning her new duties and television exposure with ABC. In negotiating her contract, Walters employed the William Morris Agency, a company known for its stable of big-name movie, television, and recording stars. The journalistic world seemed momentarily taken aback. Richard Salant, the head of CBS news, appeared upset: "I'm really depressed as hell. This isn't journalism, this is a minstrel show. Is Barbara a journalist or is she Cher?"[6] Walter Cronkite, for years the dean of the network news anchors, was equally stunned: "There was a first wave of nausea, the sickening sensation that perhaps we were all going under, that all our efforts to hold network television 147 news aloof from show business had failed."[7] Within a few years, Walters was reporting that other television journalists were thanking her. Certainly, agents to negotiate large contracts and acceptable working conditions have not only become common but an indispensable part of the television news scene. The role of the television news personality as a celebrity and a big earner for the corporation running the station is no longer in doubt. Local news anchors in major television markets now command up to $500,000 a year.

The corruption that Cronkite feared may already have set in. If so, it represents only a belated recognition that television is primarily an entertainment medium and that news reports and news programs (the "Today Show," "Good Morning America") are not public service enterprises but vital profit-making shows within the corporate structure. Economic considerations dominate television news as much as they do any other aspect of corporate business: Television is big business. Television programming is intended to bring in large amounts of money, an objective it accomplishes. In 1980, thirty-one corporations, ranging from Toyota and Anheuser-Bush to Lever Brothers and the Warner-Lambert Pharmaceutical Company, each spent over $50 million in television advertising. One corporation alone, Proctor and Gamble, invested almost $500 million in television promotion, a sum roughly approximate to the cost of all elections held in the country in 1976. Finally, television networks and stations are independent businesses that are often part of corporate empires. NBC television is, for example, but one company under the RCA umbrella, a conglomerate that owns food, car rental, recording, scientific, and defense-oriented companies among its vast $6 billion dollar holdings.[8]

To quote Richard L. Rubin:

> The network's structure, its relationship with affiliate stations and advertisers, the budget and size of the news department, as well as the percentage of "air time" devoted to news, all reflect the fact that the news is developed within an enterprise connected to profit making and, thus, the economic and organizational considerations that influence the process of news production. These considerations by a business organization determine substantially when the news is aired (and to what extent regularly

scheduled broadcasting can be interrupted for special news events), the amount of money allocated to develop the news and the range and depth of news coverage.[9]

It is a point worth bearing in mind.

◼◼◼ POLITICAL COMMERCIALS

Television news strives to be inoffensive, a fact that is not lost on viewers. In fact, Thomas E. Patterson and Robert McClure report that people receive more political information and retain it longer from thirty and sixty second political commercials than they do from news programming. There is no depth or balance to these television ads and they present little background information. They have their most pronounced effect on those who do not read newspapers regularly nor watch daily news broadcasts. Political commercials did serve to help such people become "substantially better informed."[10] "Television news makes it hard for voters to learn about issues," Patterson and McClure concluded. "When the typical election issue is mentioned infrequently, in a fleeting manner, and in a mix of extraneous news material, the almost certain result is that viewers will learn nothing about it."[11]

On the other hand, television ads have long been considered mainly as vehicles for candidate image formation. This they do, but the authors report that "our data . . . indicate that such ads convey a considerable amount of information about candidates' issues positions. In fact, messages about the issue positions of Nixon and McGovern [the study was done in the 1972 election year] were communicated more frequently through televised advertising than through television news." Overall, the televised ads constituted *"a powerful communication channel."*[12]

The Evolution of the Political Commercial

Television spots are now considered an integral part of any serious national campaign but the content and packaging of these commercials might give one pause concerning the type of knowledge that is being widely disseminated among people and then used in decision-making. For example, the 1952 presidential race saw the first widespread, although basically experimental use, of television commercials as a campaign tool. The approach of those advocating 149 this tack for the Republican presidential campaign was explained by one of the originators:

> The spots themselves would be the height of simplicity. People . . . would each ask the General [Dwight D. Eisenhower, the Republican presidential candidate] a question. . . . The General's answer would be his complete comprehension of the problem and his determination to do something about it when elected. Thus he inspires loyalty without prematurely committing himself to any straight-jacketing answer.[13]

Dwight Eisenhower followed these guidelines—showing concern but making few tangible commitments—and the age of the political spot was born. One of Eisenhower's television spots has taken its place in the political hall of fame, along with Lyndon Johnson's "daisy commercial" in 1964, and Nixon's spot on McGovern's "indecisiveness" in 1972. In the Eisenhower ad, a voice asks the general; "Mr. Eisenhower, what about the high cost of living?" The candidate replies, "My wife, Mamie, worries about the same thing. I tell her it's our job to change that on November 4."[14] Sincerity, commitment, and concern are all there, but no specific issues or solutions are discussed and no promises made. The perfect television ad!

The art has progressed since then, although it would be hard to improve on this ad. Many observers in 1976 considered the Ford television ads "brilliant," while others thought the Carter TV campaign a modern classic. The ads, unlike the campaign, were exciting.

Accentuating the Positive, or the Negative

There are "positive" and "negative" spots and most candidates use some combination of these. The positive ones extol the virtues of the presidential contender and attempt to develop a warm image for him. The negative ones attack his opponent.

Ford's positive ads in 1976 attempted to be "positive and presidential and to stick with these themes."[15] To accomplish this, Ford's television consultants devised "Oval Office" commercials, which pictured him

> . . . listening to aides, smoking his pipe, wearing a vested suit, striding through the White House,

gravely ticking off his accomplishments, presiding at
Cabinet meetings. The tone was documentary, the
colors blue and gold, the storyboards carefully
researched to address the concerns that . . . polling
surveys had shown to be on the minds of the
electorate.[16]

Incumbents (Reagan in 1984, Carter in 1980, Nixon in 1972, Johnson in 1964) often use this approach and it is effective.

Carter countered with his own positive commercials, which stressed the themes of "home," "family," "land" (Carter frequently presented himself as a farmer), and "hard work," all basic American values and all intended to show "Carter the man." In other commercials emphasizing his integrity and decency, Carter was photographed in profile speaking earnestly to the press (who remained off-camera). According to one of Carter's consultants, the message was: "Now listen to me carefully, I'll never tell a lie. I'll never make a misleading statement, I'll never avoid a controversial issue. . . . If I ever do any of these things don't support me. . . ." Later, Gerald Rafshoon, Carter's principal media advisor, added presidential-looking "symbolic" spots with the candidate in somber tie and suit speaking of his "hope" for America and the country's need for strong leadership.

The Ford people also excelled with their negative ads, often the ones to leave the most lasting impression. Ford's media specialist ran a series of six anti-Carter spots during the campaign that featured "man-in-the-street" interviews with Georgians, each of whom enumerated their reasons for disliking their former governor. One ad showed a series of Georgia newspapers endorsing Ford over Carter, all emphasizing the theme: "Those who know Jimmy Carter best are from Georgia . . . so we thought you'd like to know. . . ."[18] The best of the Ford negatives was prepared for release ten days before the November vote. It was considered so explosive that it was given "special handling" and, after reflection, not put on the air. The commercial began with a segment from one of Carter's spots. In it, Carter talked about unfair tax laws that favored the rich and then concluded, "That's disgraceful!" as the words "ACTUAL CARTER COMMERCIAL" were flashed on the screen. Edwin Diamond relates that Carter continued "to talk about tax loopholes for millionaires. Then the picture freezes over Carter's image, and the voice-over states: 'The millionare Carter family took advantage of tax loopholes to reduce 151 their taxable annual income from $135,000 to below that paid by a family of three earning $15,000 a year . . . and *that's* disgraceful.'"[19]

The same charges within the same context (discriminatory tax laws and the need to cut taxes) could have been made in the 1980 campaign with wealthy Ronald Reagan as the target. They were not. Such ads may be controversial, and when run late in a campaign, impossible to rebut. Under other conditions, they may serve as a vehicle to introduce information into the campaign debate not otherwise available. When televised, they do crystallize emotions and make an impact. Most of the negative spots have been this type of direct, uncompromising, and highly controversial ad.

Carter, of course, both in 1976 and 1980 had his own negative ad campaign. In 1976, as it turned out, they were never shown on television. In one of the 1976 ads, an actor caustically drew attention to a Republican statement on *"necessary* unemployment," and in another a voice-over listed issues Ford had taken a stand against—food stamps, day care, job training programs, school lunches, medicare—and then asked: "Who'd believe a nice man like Gerald Ford would vote against or oppose all these?"[20]

In the most publicized gaffe of the 1976 campaign, Ford denied during a televised debate that Poland and Eastern Europe were under Russian domination. It was an unfortunate position to take, but later when given the opportunity to retract the statement, Ford stubbornly refused to do so. The Carter people intended to capitalize on this—although the incident received enough publicity in its own right—by running a commercial showing Russian tanks crushing the Hungarian Revolution, while a voice asked: "Can this President of the United States be ignorant of *this?*"[21] As indicated, the Carter media advisors did not run these negative ads. They may have felt they were unnecessary.

In the 1980 prenomination campaign, however, Carter's media advisors did run a series of negative commercials in key states directed against his opponent for the Democratic party's presidential nomination, Edward Kennedy. These spots were intended to direct attention to Kennedy's unsettled personal life and may have helped in the short-run. But ultimately they appeared to have an adverse effect. Coupled with Carter's strong attacks against Reagan in the general election, they contributed to a changing perception of Jimmy Carter: He was not viewed as sympathetically as he had been. Perhaps this was inevitable, but it does highlight one of the basic weaknesses of negative ads, the danger that they can hurt the candidate they're intended to boost. Consequently, they usually aren't televised until just prior to the election, which allows them an impact while not permitting the opposition time to mount a counter-offensive, thus minimizing the backlash.

The 1980 presidential campaign made ample use of television ads. Carter, now the incumbent and fighting for his political life, attempted to exude authority and command of office, suggesting among other things that his opponent, a former movie and television actor, might be too insubstantial and impulsive to hold the position. The Carter spots also attempted to appeal to specific segments of the New Deal coalition—union members, Catholics, blacks, low income earners, big city dwellers, and ethnics— among whom Carter's popularity had declined during his four years in office.

The Reagan campaign chose to stress the personal attributes of its candidate. Reagan was presented as pleasant, likeable, reasonable, and trustworthy, and, through repeated references to his stewardship as governor of California, an experienced and competent contender for the nation's highest office. The intent was to allay suspicions of Reagan and to undercut the Carter campaign's efforts to portray him as a right-wing extremist. The ad campaign, along with a powerful boost from the last of the televised debates in particular, appears to have succeeded in its objectives.

Whatever the type of spots commissioned, or the strategy of the campaign managers in displaying them, televised ads have the greatest single impact on the viewer. They are fun. They do have something to say, often in a pointed and clever way. And people remember them. The contrast with the normal run of television and press reporting may account for their popularity and their impact.

■■■■ CONCLUSION

The media have become the major influence on and communicator during political campaigns. They have replaced the political party in this regard, further reducing the role of the party within the campaign. The most powerful and significant of the media outlets is television. It may be that television, with all its failings, is the greatest single force in politics today.

CHAPTER 12

CAMPAIGN FINANCE AND THE RISE OF PACs

■

■ RUNNING FOR OFFICE

The exercise of politics in contemporary America is very expensive, election costs having increased an average of 125 percent with each quadrennial election year. Herbert E. Alexander of the Citizens' Research Foundation estimates that the 1980 election was, in fact, the most expensive in history, costing more than a billion dollar. The presidential election alone cost a quarter of a billion dollars,[1] Ronald Reagan spending $62 million, Jimmy Carter, $56.1, and third party candidate, John B. Anderson, $12.5 million. In addition, major party candidates in the prenomination phase of the campaign spent another $700 million.

In terms of expenditures, the bulk of the Reagan and Carter general election funds went into advertising (66 percent and 56 percent respectively, up from an average of 50 percent in 1976). Reagan spent $17 million of the $29.4 million in public funds alloted to his campaign on media exposure, the Carter campaign $19.5 million of its alloted $29.4, and virtually all of that into television. The Carter-Mondale reelection committee in 1980 paid pollster Patrick H. Caddell $1 million for work done during the general election alone, while the Democratic National Committee, under Carter's direction, paid Caddell an additional $2 million for polls taken on behalf of Carter and some House and Senate candidates. In addition, Carter paid his media advisor Gerald Rafshoon another $3 million.[2] The primacy of the media consultant today is undisputed.

Congressional races are also becoming increasingly expensive. From 1974 to 1978, campaign spending rose over 100 percent (102 percent for the House, 118 percent for the Senate). The average cost of a House race rose from $54,000 to $109,000 (the latter figure is one that an election or two earlier characterized only a handful of the most expensive contexts). The average cost of a Senate race increased from $437,000 to $951,000. At the same time, the proportion of funds supplied by the political parties to congressional races (presidential contests are now funded primarily through public funds) dropped from highs in the 1972 election of 17 percent (House) and 14 percent (Senate) to an average of 6 and 5 percent for the House and Senate elections, respectively, after the adoption of the 1974 Federal Election Campaign Act and the inauguration of a modern era of campaign financing.

Where does the money come from? A congressman earns $60,662.50 a year, a little over half of what is needed to contest in an average race. Clearly, salary is not a source of campaign funding.

A candidate with personal or family wealth has enormous advantages under present conditions. In *Buckley v. Valeo* (1976), the Supreme Court struck down any restrictions on what an individual could spend on behalf of a party, a candidate, a cause, or to promote his own candidacy. The Court saw these restrictions as limitations on the First Amendment's right of free speech. The Court's decision has not greatly affected presidential elections since it allowed that when a candidate voluntarily agrees to federal campaign subsidies, he can be required to accept expenditure limits for the campaign as a whole. Since there is no federal funding of congressional elections, personal wealth can provide a significant edge in a campaign. Personal funding of congressional campaigns has risen from negligible amounts in the early seventies (1 percent or less of the total budgets) to highs of 9 percent (House) and 12 percent (Senate) by late in the decade. Individual contributions to a candidate's campaign (limited by law to a maximum of $1000) account for between 60 and 67 of the budget in recent congressional elections, with about 40 percent of this coming from contributions of $500 or more.

155

Finally, PACs have become increasingly important in funding election races, providing campaign technology, and even in recruiting candidates they wish to sponsor. As to the effect of PACs on congressional campaigns, Gary R. Orren has written that

> . . . PAC contributions are a minor factor in presidential elections. PAC contributions accounted for less than two percent of the money raised by all presidential candidates in the 1980 primaries, and represented no more than three percent of the funds raised by any single presidential candidate. PAC contributions are not matchable in the primaries and are prohibited in the general election. *As a result, PAC money has been diverted to congressional campaigns, where PAC money is far and away the fastest growing source of funds.*[3] (Italics added.)

By the late seventies, PAC contributions accounted for 25 percent of House candidates' expenditures and between 13 and 15 percent of Senate candidates' expenditures. The total money invested by PACs will continue to grow, yet, significantly, this only begins to suggest the scope of PAC influence. Through the clever use of the media, and the heavy funding of selected candidates in areas in which their opponents are particularly vulnerable, PACs have been able to maximize their influence on American elections and, consequently, on policy-making. The age of the PAC may just be dawning.

In their analysis of campaign spending in congressional races after 1974, John F. Bibby, Thomas E. Mann, and Norman J. Ornstein came to the following conclusions.
In House races—

- incumbents of both parties have a higher average level of spending than do challengers—*but the differences largely vanish in competitive races.*

- if challenger expenditures are used as an indicator of campaign effort, most House races are not seriously contested.

- both incumbent and challenger spending by Democratic and Republican candidates is concentrated in the most competitive districts, with the highest average expenditure occurring in districts lost by the incumbent.

- mean expenditures in open-seat contests are higher than the average expenditures of both Democratic and Republican incuments or challengers. This apparently reflects a view within both parties that most open seats are competitive.

- the Democrats consistently field more House candidates than do the Republicans and have a slightly higher level of total expenditures. The mean expenditures per candidate, however, show no significant differences between the parties.

In Senate races—

- incumbents in both parties normally enjoy spending advantages over their challengers, but, as in the House, they are less pronounced in competitive races.

- in both parties, the highest levels of expenditure by incumbents and challengers occur in the most competitive races.

- incumbent Republican candidates have the highest mean rate of expenditure—significantly higher than the mean Democratic expenditure.

- Democratic challengers on the average spend more than Republican challengers.

- Democratic expenditures in open seats tend to be higher than that of Republican candidates.

- although the total Republican senatorial expenditures for 1978 were significantly higher than those of the Democrats, the two parties had roughly the same financial resources in 1976, the Democrats outspending the Republicans in 1974.[4]

Despite the increasing costs of campaigning and the rising significance of new sources of funding, such as PACs, an anomaly exists. Most races are both uncompetitive *and* underfinanced. Challengers, in particular, have a difficult time attracting adequate financing since money goes to incumbents or those favored by the PACs. Approximately 60 percent of the House challengers in 1978, for example, spent less than $50,000 in their contests.

▇▇▇ REFORM AND ITS CONSEQUENCES

Election financing has been heavily regulated as a result of Watergate and the 1974 campaign act, which is not to say that there   157 were no federal restrictions on campaigns prior to 1974.[5] Early restrictions include the following:

1867 The federal antipatronage act protected federal employees from assessments for political campaigns.

1883 The Civil Service Reform Act extended protections and limitations to federal employees in relation to campaign participation.

1907 A congressional act limited national bank and corporate contributions to federal campaigns.

1910 A congressional act provided for first disclosure of funds used in federal general election campaigns.

1911 A law from the previous year was expanded to include primary, convention, and pre-election disclosure statements and limited the amount of campaign money that could be spent by House and Senate candidates. The provisions of the act regulating the pre-nomination phase were declared unconstitutional by the Supreme Court in 1921 in *Newberry v. U.S.* on the questionable grounds that the Congress's power to regulate elections did not extend to primaries and the prenomination phase. This interpretation was in itself, revised by the Supreme Court in *U.S. v. Classic* (1941), but the Congress did not again attempt to directly regulate the prenomination aspects of federal campaigns until 1972.

1925 The Federal Corrupt Practices Act, the basic law until the seventies, required the disclosure of receipts and expenditures by House and Senate candidates (although not by presidential candidates) and by political committees operating in two or more states. The law also set spending limitations for U.S. House and Senate Campaigns.

1939, 1940 The Hatch Act, passed in 1939 and amended one year later, prohibited all but top civil service employees from engaging in political activities; limited to $5000 the total contribution an individual could give to a federal candidate or political committee; instituted a sliding gift tax scale on contributions over $3,000; and extended the 1907 ban on corporate contributions.

1944, 1947 The Smith-Connally Act of 1944 applied the 1907 ban on corporate contributions to labor unions, a provision that was reenacted in the Taft-Hartley Act of 1947.

These acts were essentially unenforceable since they had numerous loopholes. Basically, they satisfied the political need to appear to legally regulate federal campaign spending while allowing a business-as-usual approach. Enforcement was lax, and except for the periodic scandals that occurred little sustained attention was given to the problems associated with political financing.

The Modern Period

The seventies saw an explosion of interest in campaign reform, a concern that was fed by the Watergate disclosures relating to the Nixon campaign of 1972. First, however, came the Revenue Act of 1971, which paved the way for the federal funding of presidential campaigns. Modern restrictions include the following:

> 1971 The Revenue Act of 1971 provided a.) for tax credits of 50 percent (up to a maximum of $12.50 for individuals or $25 for married couples filing a joint return) on federal income tax for contributions to candidates for federal, state, or local office or to certain political committees; or b.) for a tax deduction for the full amount of the contribution up to a maximum of $50 ($100 for married couples filing a joint return). The deduction provision was repealed in 1978 and the tax credit maximum was increased to $50 and $100 (for married couples) to be placed in a fund (the Presidential Election Fund) to subsidize the public financing of presidential elections, itself *not* legalized until 1974.

> 1971, 1972 The Federal Election Campaign Act (FECA) of 1971 (actually passed on January 17, 1972, a month after the Revenue Act of 1971) replaced the impotent Corrupt Practices Act of 1925 as the basic federal legislation regulating campaign funding. This law:

> ■ set limits on the amount of personal funds a candidate could invest in his own campaign, a restriction that was voided by the Supreme court. A 1976 law was then enacted that prohibited presidential candidates (only) from putting more than $50,000 in their own campaigns if they accepted public funding.

> ■ placed limits on the amount of money that a candidate (prenomination or general election) for federal office could put into the media.

159

- ■ required more specific and open disclosure proceedings.

- ■ forced all candidates and political committees to report the name, address, place of business, and occupation of each contributor of over $100, a provision bitterly resisted by both parties; and forced candidate committees to itemize every expenditure over $100 (the limits were raised to $200 in 1979).

- ■ required periodic disclosures of all contributions and expenditures (March, June, September and the 15th and 5th day before the election) prior to the election and a final campaign report by the last day in January of the succeeding year. Contributions of $5,000 or over received after the final disclosure data were to be reported within forty-eight hours of receipt. (These provisions were changed in 1974 to require quarterly disclosures, plus one 10 days before the election and a final report thirty days after.)

- ■ stipulated that a comprehensive report on national convention expenditures be filed within ninety days of its completion (previous to this such records were considered the private property of political parties).

1974 FECA (Federal Election Campaign Act) was amended to—

- ■ provide for the public funding of presidential campaigns, a major change in the assumptions that underlay campaign funding up to that point. The law subsidized the presidential contender's general election campaign (a voluntary decision in which the candidate, in return for support, agreed to strict limits on expenditures and a precise public accounting of all receipts and expenditures); provided *matching* grants for presidential prenomination races; *and granted subsidies* to the political parties for their national conventions.

- ■ create the Federal Election Commission, an independent body intended to regulate campaign funding and to provide accurate information on all aspects of federal campaign financing, realistically the first time such data were publicly available. Like the public funding of presidential elections, this marked a significant departure from previous practice.

- set expenditure limits for House and Senate campaigns (a provision later declared unconstitutional by the Supreme Court in 1976 in *Buckley v. Valeo* on the basis that, unlike presidential elections, there were no public campaign funds at stake).

- allow for the creation of PACs, a little publicized or appreciated aspect of the act at the time.

1980 FECA (Federal Election Campaign act) proposed in 1979 and signed into law in January of 1980, the amendments were designed to loosen some of the technical and filing provisions of earlier laws. These new amendments simplified and clarified previous requirements, in possibly their major contribution, permitting state and local parties increased latitude in paying for voter registration campaigns, election day get-out-the-vote drives, and in subsidizing volunteer activities.

At present, the provisions governing the financing of federal elections include the following:

Concerning Contributions

- An individual may contribute a maximum of $1,000 to a candidate in a primary or general election; the total contribution of an individual to all federal candidates is $25,000 in any one year.

- An individual can contribute a maximum of $5,000 to a political committee and $20,000 to a national party committee in a calendar year.

- A political committee can contribute a maximum of $5,000 to a candidate in an election, $15,000 to a national party committee, and $5,000 to another political committee.

- A national committee and a party's congressional campaign committee can contribute a maximum of $5,000 to a House candidate in an election and a national committee in combination with a party's senatorial campaign committee can contribute no more than $17,500 to a candidate's combined prenomination and general election campaign total.

161

- PACs are limited to a contribution of $5,000 to a candidate in an election, although they can spend as much as they want independently to promote a candidate or an issue.

- Banks, business corporations, labor unions, government contractors, and foreign nationals cannot contribute directly to federal candidates (although these organizations can work through their own specially established PACs).

- cash contributions are restricted to a maximum of $100.

Concerning Expenditures

- Presidential candidates are limited to expenditures of $10 million in prenomination campaigns and $20 million in general election campaigns (plus cost-of-living allowances) with specific spending limits per state, depending on the size of the state's electorate.

- A presidential or vice-presidential candidate who agrees to accept public funding for his campaign cannot spend more than $50,000 of his own money on the election.

- The national parties can spend 2 cents per voter on their campaign (almost $4 million per party).

- The party's national committee and its House and Senate campaign committees can jointly spend up to $10,000 on House campaigns and $20,000 on Senate campaigns (or 2 cents for each state's voting age population in Senate elections, whichever is the greater amount), plus cost-of-living allowances on behalf of House or Senate candidates.

- State parties can spend the same amount on behalf of U.S. House and Senate candidates.

- There are *no* limits on how much a House or Senate campaign can receive or spend; on how much individuals or groups can spend on behalf of a House or Senate candidate, or on behalf of a presidential candidate, if done *independently* of the individual campaign (i.e., the expenditure cannot represent a concerted effort by the group or individual in concert with the candidate or his campaign committee); and there is no limit on the amount of personal funds a House or Senate candidate can invest in his own campaign (all as a result of *Buckley v. Valeo*, 1976).

Concerning the Public Financing of Presidential Campaigns

- The Republican and Democratic parties; presidential nominees receive $20 million (plus inflation and cost-of-living increases, an amount that totalled $29.4 million in 1980) for their general election campaigns; participation in the program is voluntary, but those who do participate cannot accept private contributions.

- Third parties qualify for public funding of their presidential campaigns in proportion to the number of votes they receive in the election *if* 1. they receive 5 percent of the vote in the previous presidential election, or, 2. for a new third party, if they receive 5 percent of the vote in the election, with the money to be paid *after* the election.

- To qualify for matching public funding of up to $5 million (plus cost-of-living adjustments) in primaries and prenomination campaigns, presidential candidates of the major parties must raise $100,000 in private contributions ($5,000 of which must be raised in contributions no larger than $250 in 20 states) to show support and a geographical appeal to a candidacy and, not incidentally, to keep from funding "favorite son" candidacies; above $100,000, each candidate receives matching federal funds for each contribution of up to $250 he receives; no candidate may claim more than 25 percent of the total available funds.

- In order to discourage hopeless prenomination campaigns, presidential candidates who receive less than 10 percent of the vote in two successive primaries lose their public funding.

- The national parties (and to a lesser extent the third and minor parties that qualify by receiving a minimum level of the popular vote) receive federal funds to conduct their national conventions.

Concerning Administration of the Campaign Laws

- All candidate and campaign committees must have one centralized committee and procedure to monitor receipts and expenditures and to file the necessary, periodic disclosure reports.

- The Federal Election Commission supervises federal campaign receipts, expenditures and disclosures, and compliance 163 with the laws and administers and allocates the funding of the specified campaigns; it also has the power to initiate civil actions through the courts; to serve as a depository for all reports, and to publicize its findings.

The 1980 campaign was the most heavily regulated and thoroughly scrutinized in history. By 1980, the public funding of presidential campaigns was well established and apparently was popular with the voters, and there was a move under consideration (as there had been since the initiation of federal campaign subsidies) to extend public financing to House and Senate races (a move resisted by the Congress and the PACs).

Funding Changes in Perspective

The recent laws have improved the manner in which campaigns are regulated and have reasserted the public's interest in, and control over, campaign financing. Public subsidization of a vital aspect of the elective process—the selection of a president—is now a reality, which was unthinkable a generation ago. Generally, the new practice has been accepted, and even enthusiastically supported, by the public, candidates for office, and both political parties.

This is not to say that candidates are satisfied with present practices. While candidates and the parties are pleased to accept public campaign funds, they are irritated by the accounting and disclosure procedures contained in the more recent campaign acts. As well, the candidate organizations and the Congress are wary of the Federal Election Commission and its supervision of campaign practices. As one FEC member noted, the Congress is ambivalent about the FEC's powers and its role: "Congress wants to be able to point to a campaign watchdog, but they don't want it to do anything. Our enemies in Congress would like to abolish us. Their second choice is to castrate us." Since its inception, there have been repeated attempts to strip the FEC of most of its enforcement powers and to place its operation under closer congressional scrutiny.

Candidates for public office do have grounds for complaint. Many of the actual enforcement procedures are overly technical and detailed and the FEC has been particularly slow, to the point of negligence, in processing some of the cases before it (for example, the long-running investigation of Bert Lance—a Georgia

banker and Carter supporter who resigned as director of the Bureau of the Budget after allegations surfaced of improper bank loans to his 1974 gubernatorial campaign—and its investigation into $43,000 of unaccounted expenditures for the 1976 presidential prenomination campaign of Congressman Morris Udall ("How do you track down a college volunteer who spent $47 to make copies of some newspaper clips and didn't think to get a receipt?" complained one campaign official)[6]

Still, the problems with the newer laws and the performance of the FEC are relatively minor. The intent of the laws and the new age of publicly-governed and publicly-accountable campaign processes are to be welcomed.

▇▇▇ THE COMING AGE OF THE PACs

The increase in the number of PACs since their legitimization in the 1974 campaign act has been spectacular (Table 12.1). They have quickly become one of the most prominent avenues for funding campaigns and for representing the views of corporations, unions, trade associations, dairy cooperatives, and any other group with the financial base and organizational know-how to make an impact on the political process. The number of PACs has increased from a total of 608 at the end of 1974 to 2,551 by 1980. Most significantly, while the number of union PACs has shown only a modest rise (96 new ones were created during this period), the number of corporate PACs mushroomed from 89 in 1974 to over 1200 by 1980 (Table 12.1). According to Edwin M. Epstein, the increasing number and political activity of the PACs may represent only "the tip of a possible iceberg."[7] We have just begun to realize what their role in American politics could be.

The PACs and the Parties

Many concerns have been voiced about PACs: It is feared they will replace the parties in funding and in providing technical expertise in key races of concern to them and that they will recruit and run their own candidates for public office, whatever the cost to the political parties or to the less definable but nonetheless real public interest. But it appears this has already happened. Ideological PACs claim credit for the defeat of such prominent political figures as Senators Dick Clark (Dem.) and John Culver (Dem.) of Iowa; George McGovern (Dem.) of South Dakota; Frank 165

TABLE 12.1 ■ PAC Growth, 1974–1980

Committee Type[a]	12/31/74	12/31/76	12/31/77	12/31/78	12/31/79	12/31/80	Ratio Increment 1974–1980
Corporate	89	433	538	784	949	1204	13.53 times
Labor	201	224	216	218	240	297	1.48 times
Trade associations							
Membership organizations	318	489	544	631	811	1050	3.3 times
Cooperatives							
Corporations w/out capital stock							
Other							
Total	608	1146	1298	1633	2000	2551	4.2 times

Source: Federal Election Commission as reported in Ann B. Matasar, "Corporate Responsibility Gone Awry?: The Corporate Political Action Committee," a paper delivered at the Annual Meeting of the American Political Science Association, 1981.
[a] All committees are classified as to their connected organization. The Trade, Membership category may include incorporated trade associations or membership organizations, corporations without capital stock, cooperatives, and other organizations.

Church (Dem.) of Idaho; Thomas McIntyre (Dem.) and David Durkin (Dem.) of New Hampshire; Gaylord Nelson (Dem.) of Wisconsin; Jacob Javits (Rep.) of New York; Warren Magnuson (Dem.) of Washington; and Birch Bayh (Dem.) of Indiana. PAC-recruited primary opponents reputedly weakened the reelection campaigns of Senators Edward W. Brooke (Rep.) of Massachusetts, who eventually lost in the general election to a Democrat, and Clifford Case of New Jersey, who was beaten in a low-turnout Republican primary by a young, right-wing ideologue (Jeffrey Bell). The challenge of a conservative, PAC-supported minister reportedly contributed to Illionis Republican John Anderson's decision to retire from the House to seek the Republican party's nomination for the presidency (eventually, of course, running as an independent).

Most of the incumbents opposed are moderate, centrists, or liberal Democrats and Republicans. Most of the candidates recruited or supported tend to be extremely conservative (Deaton of Alabama, Helms and East of North Carolina, Humphrey of New Hampshire, Grassley and Jepsen of Iowa, Symms of Idaho, Nickles of Oklahoma, Kasten of Wisconsin, Abdnor of South Dakota, Quayle of Indiana, Hawkins of Florida). The result is an emerging conservatism among public office holders that may or may not reflect the views of the voters. These elections do suggest the emerging power of the PACs, though.

The PACs and Campaign Funding

A second area of concern is the volume of money being pumped into the political system through the PACs and its distribution to incumbents and, disproportionately, to Republicans in open and/or competitive races. If such trends continue, then the dominant thrust of PACs may have far-reaching policy consequences.

It is difficult to trace the exact distribution and impact of funds. An examination of the top fifty PACs (actually fifty-one in terms of contributions) in the Chicago area indicated that virtually all concentrate in varying proportions on national races (Table 12.2). The few that confine their activities within the state (the Illinois Medical Association, Illinois Bell) have their major policy interests best served by such decisions. They also are associated with national PACs that work on behalf of their broader interest.

Only two of the top fifty PACs are union-related (Nos. 38 and 47) in an area that is heavily unionized and highly industrial-   167

TABLE 12.2 ■ Contributions of the Major Chicago Area PACs, 1979–1980: Amount of Contribution, Party Supported, and Level of Race (National/State)

Rank	Sponsor	Contribution	Dem/GOP%[a]	Illinois Races (% of all races)
1.	National Assn. of Realtors	$1,541,573	(48/52)	5
2.	Chicago Mercantile Exchange	274,075	(40/60)	10
3.	Dart & Kraft Inc.[b]	242,954	(13/87)	5
4.	Standard Oil Co. (Ind.)	193,950	(21/78)	7
5.	Chicago Board of Trade	136,899	(69/30)	15
6.	Sears, Roebuck and Co.	104,575	(21/79)	6
7.	McDonald's Corp.	98,650	(20/80)	9
8.	FMC Corp.	95,225	(37/62)	6
9.	Chicago & North Western Transportation Co.	93,600	(54/45)	10
10.	UAL Inc.	79,000	(53/46)	11
11.	Illinois Medical Assn.	74,536	(24/76)	100
12.	Belden Corp.	74,200	(14/86)	9
13.	Abbott Laboratories	73,012	(25/74)	10
14.	American Hospital Assn.	72,306	(48/52)	6
15.	Motorola Inc.	65,891	(38/61)	11
16.	American Assn. of Oral and Maxillofacial Surgeons	59,000	(61/39)	7
17.	Interlake Inc.	54,308	(23/73)	26
18.	Household International Inc.	44,550	(37/62)	12
19.	National Assn. of Insurers	41,250	(33/67)	71
20.	International Harvester Co.	40,905	(25/75)	24
21.	Gould Inc.	39,325	(43/57)	15
22.	Square D Co.	36,250	(5/95)	5
23.	Sundstrand Corp.	34,379	(0/96)	27

continued

TABLE 12.2 ■ Continued

Rank	Sponsor	Contribution	Dem/ GOP%[a]	Illinois Races (% of all races)
24.	Citizens Concerned for the National Interest	33,000	(14/86)	14
25.	Archer Daniels Midland Co.	32,400	(41/59)	36
26.	Brunswick Corp.	30,000	(21/79)	45
27.	International Minerals & Chemical Corp.	29,500	(56/44)	10
28.	R. R. Donnelley & Sons Co.	29,113	(13/84)	13
29.	IC Industries Inc.	24,985	(51/47)	40
30.	Santa Fe Industries Inc.	23,715	(36/64)	36
31.	Chicago Board Options Exchange	23,250	(41/59)	35
32.	Deere & Co.	23,050	(9/91)	31
33.	Amsted Industries Inc.	22,000	(0/100)	16
34.	G. D. Searle & Co.	21,100	(33/67)	33
35.	Kemper Insurance Cos.	20,500	(12/88)	22
	Quaker Oats Co.	20,500	(19/81)	32
36.	Chicago Milwaukee Corp.	19,050	(62/28)	20
37.	Borg-Warner Corp.	18,625	(18/82)	22
38.	Amalgamated Clothing and Textile Workers-Chicago	18,250	(100/0)	25
39.	Balcor Co.	16,000	(92/8)	8
40.	Illinois Tool Works Inc.	15,025	(15/85)	42
41.	Edward Hines Lumber Co.	14,825	(21/79)	33
42.	A. E. Staley Manufacturing Co.	14,800	(12/88)	23
43.	Morton Buildings Inc.	14,750	(7/93)	13

continued

TABLE 12.2 ■ Continued

Rank	Sponsor	Contribution	Dem/ GOP%[a]	Illinois Races (% of all races)
44.	CBI Industries Inc.	14,200	(8/92)	5
45.	CF Industries Inc.	12,500	(44/56)	6
46.	Illinois Bell Telephone Co.	12,100	(30/70)	100
47.	Brotherhood of Railroad Signalmen	11,850	(100/0)	8
48.	Inland Steel Co.	11,750	(15/85)	30
49.	Waste Management Inc.	11,550	(41/59)	29
50.	First Chicago Corp.	11,450	(58/42)	58

Source: Federal Election Commission as reported in Paul Merrion, "Illinois PACs Pose Tough Choices in '82 Races," *Crain's Chicago Business*, January 25, 1982.
[a] Contributions to third party candidates account for some totals below 100%.
[b] Includes $228,229 in PAC contribution from Dart Industries, Inc., prior to Dart's merger with Kraft in 1980.

ized. The rest represent well-known names in American business (Sears, United Airlines, Motorola, McDonald's, Standard Oil), financial institutions, trade associations (surgeons, realtors, insurance agents), railroads, the construction industry, pharmaceuticals, and the like. Eighty percent give the majority of their funds to Republicans and one-half of these contribute 70 percent or more of their money to the Republican party. Overall, Republicans have a two-to-one edge in PAC receipts among the top fifty Chicago givers.

The significance of this distribution can readily be seen. Local corporations, dependent on the goodwill of a Democratic city administration, contribute disproportionately to local Democrats. This is an old political tradition that is savored in Chicago. At the national level, the two union PACs also gave all their funds to the Democratic party. Prior to 1974, under law, the unions were the only ones allowed to maintain PACs, an advantage to the Democrats. Since then, and with a better than ten-to-one increase in the number of corporate PACs, Republicans and more conservative candidates have benefitted.

This trend may not be as self-evident as it seems. At one point in the 1978 congressional campaign, it appeared that the Democrats, then controlling both houses of the Congress, would do far better in the proportion of PAC funds they attracted than had been anticipated.[8] This reflected what Edward Handler and

John Mulkern refer to as a "pragmatic" approach to campaign funding: give to incumbents in hopes that you will be remembered in times of need. The approach is quite effective. It was challenged, however, by Donald M. Kendall of Pepsico (Pepsi Cola) who, in a letter to his fellow members of the Business Round Table (a prestigious and influential representative of corporate interests) questioned whether it was better to serve long-run ideological concerns by supporting those most sympathetic to a business philosophy rather than the short-run interests of a corporation's Washington lobbyist.[9] It would hardly seem that a corporate PAC could lose either way, and many fund both types of candidates. Still, it would appear that a strategy emphasizing a commitment to long-term ideological gains is receiving a more sympathetic hearing.

An examination of PAC contributions during the seventies revealed that labor gave predominantly to Democrats (except in hopeless contests), a not surprising finding; business gave disproportionately to Republicans in competitive and non-competitive races, with the reservation that Republicans facing safe Democratic incumbents were not considered good investments; conservative ideological PACs generally paralleled business PACs in their choice of candidates they contributed to although they did tend to concentrate funding more on competitive races and in attempts to defeat highly visible liberal incumbents in a select number of targeted races.[10]

These are the general trends, but there are other aspects to PAC contributions that are less obvious. Senate incumbents who were not seriously challenged, for example, and who spent less than the norm on their reelection campaigns still received sizeable PAC donations in line with those given to candidates in close races. In the noncompetitive races, PAC funds represented a disproportionately high share (20 percent or more of the total receipts) of the money collected by the incumbents.[11]

Are PACs Irresponsible?

Another and possibly even more worrisome aspect associated with the rise of PACs has been their accountability, or more accurately, lack of accountability in campaigns. Not only are they well funded and of increasing significance in campaigns and not only is there a pattern to their contributions that has consequences for policymaking and the representativeness of the system, but the PACs 171 themselves are directly answerable to no one. They do not necessarily represent anyone or account for their actions to anyone, a fact that does not diminish their influence. These concerns are directed more to the ideological and single issue PACs—a highly visible part of American political life in recent years—than they are to corporate, trade, or labor PACs since the ideological and single issues PACs specialize in negative campaigning. They come into a locality—ostensibly unrelated to, and unrestrained by any ties to, any party or candidate—and unremittingly attack their target, primarily through paid media commercials. The PAC can make charges that in another context might be hard to prove or defend. In the heat of a campaign, whatever their basis in fact, these changes are difficult to answer or counter. As a consequence, they can be very effective.

An Indiana journalist, commenting on the New Right's PAC campaign against Democratic Senator Birch Bayh in 1980, remarked, "I don't think there's been anything comparable to this. Here's a group [NCPAC, the National Conservative Political Action Committee] that comes in and isn't even supporting, isn't even favoring his opponent [but] just wants to get Bayh."[12] It did. An official of Senator Frank Church's campaign in Idaho said, "I've never seen a campaign like this before in Idaho, a campaign where a single group has just been attacking one man's integrity for a year and a half, just stabbing away."[13] Again, it was effective.

The tactics are rough, but they succeed. In fact, they work so well that the left has fielded its first ideological PAC (PROPAC, the Progressive Political Action Committee) intent on adopting the strategies of the conservative ideological PACs, which have had the field to themselves until now. Their objective is to confront the New Right PACs on their own ground. Not everyone is comfortable with such an approach and the results are not likely to prove uplifting to the tone and conduct or campaign debates. Nonetheless, it matters little. The PACs are free to do as they please. As one of its cofounders said: "PROPAC is basically Harnet [Matthews, formerly of the National Abortion Rights Action League] and myself and a handful of other people whose names nobody would know."[14]

While its budget ($200,000) is minuscule compared to the multimillion dollar budget of NCPAC and other conservative ideological PACs, its tactics are familiar. It has targeted such stalwarts of the right as Republican Senators Jesse Helms of North Carolina, Orrin Hatch of Utah, and Jack Schmitt of New Mexico. A PRO-

PAC newspaper advertisement on Helms read: "If you think Jesse Helms is against Big Government, Think Again!" The ad contended that Helms, through legislation, wanted "to dictate the most private family planning decisions of a husband and wife." "To keep government and Jesse Helms out of your bedroom," it continued, "you must first get Jesse Helms out of the Senate."[15] A Hatch ad read: "When Orring Hatch says he likes the Houston Oilers, he's not talking about football. . . .When Orrin Hatch cries 'Wolf,' big business sends money."[16] A Schmitt ad claiming that the only bill the Senator had passed was to reimburse oil developers for money lost on a sublease, read: "Jack Schmitt may not get much done in the Senate, but he looks good doing it."[17] PROPAC'S director claims that, unlike its opponents, the NCPAC in particular, it will not resort to "lies, distortions and fearmongering."[18] Of course, that is exactly the type of charge that has been directed against such ideological PACs in the past. Future campaigns are likely to see more, not less, of the same.

◼◼◼ CONCLUSION

PACs of all varieties will probably continue to play a disproportionately visible role in the conduct of campaigns. As to corporate PACs, Edwin M. Epstein predicts that their membership will continue to grow, that in the early eighties their receipts might increase to as much as $40–$50 million, "with contributions of $25–30 million to congressional candidates . . . moreover, at least some companies will begin to undertake new forms of electoral involvement such as automatic payroll deduction, nonpartisan registration, get-out-the-vote drives, and internal political communication among managerial level employees and shareholders. . . . these projections of future corporate PAC operations [are] . . . conservative estimates and not reckless speculations."[19]

Concerning ideological PACs, and especially those of the New Right, Richard A. Viguerie (one of their founding fathers) is bullish. Viguerie believes that the battle, while highly successful to date, has just begun. After accusing the left of everything from allowing "ruthless Communist takeovers in Vietnam, Laos, Cambodia, and Afghanistan" to favoring "the non-producers over the people who work" to encouraging "American women to feel that they are failures if they want to be wives and mothers,"[20] he declares:

173

The liberals had a lot of victories over the last 50 years. But they've grown soft and sluggish. They have lost confidence in themselves and in their ideas.

We're lean, determined and hungry—to gain victories for conservatism and to renew our great country.

Yes, the tide is turning. It is turning our way—freedom's way.[21]

But our final triumph won't happen automatically. All the conditions are favorable. But we still have to *make* it happen, just as much as when we set out, many years ago, to fight our first lonely battles.[22]

It promises to be an interesting decade.

CHAPTER 13

CONCLUSION: REVISIONIST THOUGHTS ON POLITICAL PARTIES

The research on political parties, while extensive, is inconclusive. It follows a multiplicity of conceptual lines and examines few questions in any depth or in any cumulative fashion. Much of it represents a pleasant distraction of incidental concern to developing a body of generalized, scientifically verifiable propositions that *explain* party behavior and relate it to its environment. As a consequence of the conflicting conceptual and methodological approaches employed in the research, a general anarchy prevails in the field (not unlike the subject matter of the party specialist's concern itself). Much of what passes for party explorations are speculative or ideological pieces that mask hidden values on the way in which political parties, and society more generally, *should* operate.

In many respects, research in political parties is at least a generation out-of-date. Assumptions have been deified; conclusions of earlier research pieces or investigators have been taken as immutable; and academic energies have been given over to arguing why such propositions either continue to be relevant or *should* be relevant, despite evidence to the contrary. Considerably less attention is devoted to in-depth, empirical investigations of party structures, operations, and the environmental and cultural forces that affect these at different points in time. It is all good, clean 175 fun, but a price is paid. The cost is, of course, a true understanding of political parties as social institutions of enormous consequence to the political system.

Times have changed and they will continue to change. This much should be evident from a reading of this book. The political parties have *not* adapted well to date: What does the future hold? It is extremely difficult, given the improbability of predicting future social developments coupled with the absence of a reliable, systematic data base on the parties, to say much with any degree of assurance. Nonetheless, several models of potential alternative choices facing the party system may help to clarify the possibilities.

With editorial comments included as guides, the four schools of thought relevant to today's political parties are as follows:

■■■■ THE "LET THEM EAT CAKE" SCHOOL

This school has perhaps the dominant commitment among political scientists content with unarticulated assumptions concerning what a party system represented. It is a partly whimsical and partly accurate, at least in its view of how the parties operated, although its arguments concerning the beneficial consequences of party operations are suspect. Needless to say, the approach is backward-looking and romanticized, with an emphasis on idealizing a party system that never was.

Basically, the idea is that the parties that operated during the New Deal of the thirties and forties up through the sixties were the best conceivable and served well the needs of a democratic polity. While admitting, when pressed, the failings of the party system of this era, proponents of this point of view advance a number of arguments. One was that they were aberrations (severe, long-lasting, but aberrations nonetheless). Another was the failings represented a tolerable price to pay for the overall performance of the system. Amother defense was simply to claim that they do not exist, thus, they were only in the eye and mind of the beholder. Or that, whatever its failings, the New Deal party system—or some mutation of it (a Daley-like Chicago machine operation nationwide)—was immensely preferable to any alternative that could be devised. Usually, "all of the above," offered as a package, constituted the basic defense.

The party system envisioned by these advocates has little room for people in general, or party supporters or voters more specifically. Decisions on policy choices and nominees for office are made by a coterie of leaders, in this case, big city mayors and industrial state governors, public office holders, and the major interest group leaders (such as the AFL-CIO's George Meaney). The role of the party member or voter is restricted primarily to passing on the issue and candidate choices offered by the party's elite in the general election. If a voter or party member did not like the offerings, he could vote for the (probably equally unattractive) choices offered by the opposition or refrain from voting altogether. The system was not a model of democratic decision-making or inclusiveness. That it has had trouble surviving in the contemporary age should not be surprising.

That such a system could prove unresponsive and cut-off from its base, as it was during the Vietnam era, with the attendant social, political, and human consequences, is of little relevance. This, its advocates say, was one of the aberrations in its performance that is generally acknowledged but dismissed as transitory. That such a system proved unworkable and that it has become a casualty of changing times, an alternative that cannot be returned to, is a more difficult argument to refute. In fact, it cannot be answered. The era of the quasi-closed New Deal party system, whatever its strengths or weaknesses, is over. It does not represent a viable possibility for the future. Many of the changes in party services and structures over the last decade have represented efforts to deal with, and overcome, some of the least desirable side effects of the old party system, many of which continue to linger on.

▣ BRITISH TRANSPLANT SCHOOL

This model is a hybrid based on a corruption or simplified perception of the British party system, which can trace its origins back to such notable early advocates as A. Laurence Lowell and Woodrow Wilson. Since those days, it has been a persistent reform alternative that has been advocated as the main point of departure for those primarily academic critics of the American party system. It calls for "responsible" parties, ones which put forth coherent policy proposals to the electorate and ones that have the cohesion and discipline necessary to enact the programs once in office that the parties commit themselves to in elections. The emphasis is on a policy dimension that links votes, candidates, and policy programs through a strong party structure.

It is an enticing idea. The fact that it has been around so long, bitterly criticized (as well as warmly supported) by political scientists, while ignored by the practicing politician, suggests it is in reality an untenable alternative, not terribly relevant to the American experience. Nonetheless, it is being revived, and has acquired increasing support, in the waning days of the elitist, coalitional bargaining system of the New Deal era. In fact, many, who formerly attacked the British Transplant model as something of an unwelcome and utopian intrusion on the American scene, have in recent years viewed it more sympathetically. Possibly, they see it as the only kid on the block, if you recognize a need for change and admit to the failings of the coalitional group compromise approach of the old party system. Still, it is as unrealistic in the eighties as it was in the forties or the early nineteen-hundreds.

The British Transplant model does include some of the more attractive aspects—at least, as seen from a distance—of the British system. The policy cohesiveness and party accountability aspects of the approach have a decided appeal and, if they could be enacted, would address one of the major weaknesses in the American party system. Such a change also should appeal to an electorate that is increasingly issue-oriented and less reliant on traditional party loyalties. The problem is two-fold. The British system works moderately well in the United Kingdom, but whether it would do equally well in a country thirty-eight times larger, with a population four times greater, operating under a federalized government, a checks and balances division of political responsibility, and a presidential system of leadership (as opposed to a unitary governing arrangement and parliamentary system) is another matter. To date, it has not proven transferable and nothing in the future is likely to change sufficiently to accommodate itself to such a party arrangement. The British model is not adaptable to the United States. Each nation's party system is a direct outgrowth of its needs, traditions, and political structures. Within such a context, the British model ill-fits the demands of the American system.

The major brief advocating an adaptive form of the British approach is the report *Towards a Responsible Two Party System*,, published by the American Political Science Association in 1950.[1] A close reading of this report leaves one a little bewildered. Assuming the value of a "responsible" parties' approach and the desirability of a cohesive policy orientation in party appeals, *there is*

nothing in the institutions the report advocates that would insure such an outcome. Put another way, the two major parties could adopt many, if not all, of the policy conferences, party agendas, and other ideas advocated in the report and not substantially change the nature or workings of the American party system. To a degree, this has happened: The Democrats have midterm policy conferences; both parties (the Democrats only recently) sponsor retreats for their elective officials to review and agree upon policy assumptions; the Republican National Committee has become a highly professionalized, well-funded, and aggressive resource center for Republicans nationally; the state parties appear to be more institutionalized and better organized than they were a generation ago; the party caucuses in the House and Senate have acquired new meaning in defining each party's legislative positions and in demanding minimal standards of party conduct in the Congress; and the seniority system in the Congress has weakened with the parties exercising a final and decisive say in committee and chair appointments. Many developments have taken place that should have had an impact on the overall operations of the American parties, strengthening them and moving them in the direction of pro-party responsibility.

In the fifties, these changes would have been welcomed as highly desirable reforms and, unquestionably, they represent improvements in the manner in which the parties operate. Such modifications are to be valued, but they have not affected the basic nature of the party system. Both parties remain undisciplined, inchoate masses, responsive to organized political interests, with little voting coherence on even the most critical issues (from Vietnam to budget priorities, economic recovery plans, or "New Federalism" alternatives). The party system remains the same laissez-faire, every-candidate-for-himself, amorphous marshmallow that it has been in the past. A "responsible" party system seems as far away, and as unsuited to the American political climate, now as it always has. A permutation of the British system would not appear to be the answer.

THE POPULIST MODEL

This school has its recent roots in the party reform movement of the seventies. What its proponents hoped for was a revitalized party system sensitive to the policy needs of a nation in flux, with open parties emphasizing participation in their activities and de- 179 cision-making by party members. Real power would rest with a party's grassroots membership and from all of this world emerge a party accountable and responsive to its local constituencies. It was presumed that such an open, issue-concerned, and democratic party arrangement would offer a meaningful alternative to the self-aggrandizing, insular party system in operation and the insensitivity of a party system seemingly out-of-touch with, and at times even scornful of, its base constituency.

The major success of the participant-oriented Populist model came in the adoption of new rules to guide presidential selection within the Democratic party during the early seventies, a move that eventually affected both parties.[2] It can be argued that the present party system is actually a hybrid mix of assumptions and models, with a Populist base in presidential selection, a let-them-eat-cake approach to most state, local, and national party operations, laden with occasional strains pirated from the British Transplant model (the policy conferences and other institutional modifications adopted in recent years).[3]

There was an effort in the mid-seventies to superimpose the Populist initiative developed in presidential selection—open party structures, grassroots accountability, and due process guarantees for participants—on the national party organizations. An ambitious restructuring within the Democratic party's national hierarchy took place, but the operations, power concentrations, and representativeness of the post-reform party are not strikingly dissimilar from its pre-reform antecedents. The Populist model has made inroads on the conduct of party affairs and in the thinking concerning the future of the parties. Whether such an approach will proceed much beyond where it rests now, whether it has arrived too late to significantly alter the decline in party status, or whether it offers the sole, or even the most reasonable, alternative to the parties' dilemma can all serve as the focal points for prolonged debate.

■■■ THE "PARTIES-AS-A-PLEASANT-MEMORY" ALTERNATIVE

This may be where we are, or at least close to where we are, today. In an age dominated by television and the media, PACs and single issue groups, demanding ideological associations, excessive funding, a disgruntled electorate, a personalized politics, and the lack
of a disciplined, core opposition, parties as such may be just pleas-

urable symbolic association with the past. The parties and party labels have not disappeared. They continue on, but are of little relevance in recruiting candidates or as influences on voters. The parties remain but they are of little consequence to the resolution of issues of the day. They perform some functions—for example, providing the institutional framework in which party nominees are selected and in supplying supplemental campaign services—but they are not of core concern to the conduct of political life. Political decisions—by the individual or the candidate—are made in isolation and in a consideration of their own needs. The major channels of influence and information dispersed are the media. Political parties are tolerated, but ignored. A gentle nihilism prevails, with little accountability of political leaders, rapid and severe departures in policy programs from one administration to the next, little predictability in the vote, and a continuingly alienated electorate. It is all quite familiar. We may not be at this point yet, but such a "no-party" age may not be far off.

■ CONCLUSION

The contrast presented among the models is stark, possibly more so than actual conditions warrant. The present situation finds aspects of all represented in a party system that has lost its way. It may be that the realignment—long anticipated by political scientists—will yet come to pass. The issues and personalities that could trigger such a monumental political restructuring have not yet appeared. Even should it occur, the difficulties that have plagued the last party system would most likely continue and the debate over party deficiencies might well develop much as it did in the past.

Most of the contemporary energies of party scholars and the practicing politicians appear directed to returning the political parties to something that they never were, an ideal that has never, and could never, exist. A more fruitful approach would be to attempt to understand the present and to adapt the parties to an environment radically transformed in the last few decades, one in which they must compete. Efforts would be better directed toward anticipating the future and its needs and what (and how) the political parties can contribute to these, rather than to attempting to justify, or resurrect, that which has gone before. 181

Notes

▬

Chapter 1. Public Attitudes and Party Support

1. See Arthur Miller, 1974.

2. See Miller, Miller, and Schneider, pp. 259–62, 275, 278.

3. Jensen, 1981, pp. 84–85.

4. Dennis, 1975, p. 187.

5. Ibid., p. 189.

6. See Miller, Miller, and Schneider, p. 256.

7. Dennis, 1980, pp. 55–56.

8. Ibid., p. 60.

9. Ibid., p. 62.

10. Schattschneider, 1942, p. 1.

11. Burnham, 1976, p. 431.

Chapter 2. Political Participation and Voter Turnout

1. Cavanagh, 1979.

2. Burnham, 1979.

3. Wolfinger and Rosenstone, 1980.

4. See also Axelrod, 1972.

5. Wolfinger and Rosenstone, 1980, pp. 106–107, 110.

6. Various explanations of the decline can be found in Cavanagh, 1981; Wolfinger and Rosenstone, 1980; Abramson and Aldrich, 1981; and Crotty, 1980c.

7. For governors, see Luttbeg, 1981.

8. Ibid, p. 8.

9. See sources in note 6 above.

10. See Crotty, 1984, pp. 142–186.

11. Stanley, 1981.

12. Cohen, Cotter, and Coulter, 1981, p. 11.

13. Crotty, 1984, pp. 142–186.

14. Schattschneider, 1960.

15. Burnham, 1979, p. 63.

Chapter 3. The Nature of Party Competition

1. Sellers, 1965. See also Burnham, 1970; Andersen, 1979; Campbell and Trilling, 1980; and Petrocik, 1981.

2. Fee, 1980.

3. Sundquist, 1973; Campbell and Trilling, 1980.

4. Burnham, 1970; Ladd and Hadley, 1975.

5. See Ornstein, Mann, Malbin, and Bibby, 1982, pp. 38–39.

6. Ibid., pp. 46–47.

7. Ibid., p. 42.

8. Ibid., p. 50. See also Mann, 1978; and Cover and Mayhew, 1981.

9. See Chapter 9.

10. For a discussion of this phenomenon, see Bass and DeVries, 1977; and Havard, 1972.

11. Burnham, 1976, pp. 472–473.

12. See Ladd, 1976–77.

Chapter 4. Third Parties and Their Contributions to the Party System

1. For general background and an introduction to the literature on third parties and the extensive historical works on individual third parties, see Mazmanian, 1974; Rosenstone, Behr, and Lazarus, 1981; and Penniman, 1980.

2. Federal law limits contributions to a maximum of $1,000 for candidates and $20,000 for political parties. The two major parties are subsidized by federal funds during the election as is any third or minor party that received over 5 percent of the vote in the previous election. When a third or minor party attracts 5 percent or more of the vote for the first time, it receives its proportionate share of federal funds after the election. The major parties (and any other party that has previously qualified) receive theirs prior to the election.

3. Penniman, 1980.

4. Personal communication.

5. Kleppner, 1981.

6. Burnham, 1976, p. 475.

7. Mazmanian, 1974, pp. 81–82.

8. Ibid., p. 82.

Chapter 5. Party Loyalty and Election Outcomes

1. Converse, 1976.

2. Nie, Verba, and Petrocik, 1976, pp. 47–48.

3. Ibid., p. 48.

4. The literature on this point is extensive. See, as examples, Asher, 1980; Petrocik, 1981; Brody and Page, 1972; Margolis, 1977; Page, 1978; Pomper, 1975; Fiorina, 1981; Key, 1966; Campbell, Converse, Miller, and Stokes, 1960; Jackson, 1975; Miller, Miller, Raine, and Brown, 1976; Miller and Wattenberg, 1981; Miller and Miller, 1977; and Nie, Verba, and Petrocik, 1976.

5. Miller, Miller, Raine, and Brown, 1976, p. 190.

6. Ibid., pp. 191–192.

Chapter 6. Party Loyalty and Recent Elections

1. Miller, 1917, pp. 131–132.

2. Ibid., p. 150.

3. Ibid., p. 141.

4. Ibid., pp. 131–133.

5. Quoted in Crotty, 1980a.

6. Quoted in Pomper, 1981, p. 84.

7. Ibid., p. 88.

8. Ibid.

9. See Schneider, 1981, pp. 254, 256.

10. Robinson, 1981; Frankovic, 1981; Wirthlin, 1981; Caddell, 1981; Burnham, 1981; Ponper, 1981; and Abramson, Aldrich, and Rhode, 1982.

11. Crotty, 1980a.

12. Pomper, 1981, p. 3. An assessment of economic policies in the campaign can be found in McDonald, 1981.

13. Markus, 1981, pp. 11–12.

184 **14.** Schneider, 1981, p. 241.

15. Crotty, 1980a.

16. W. Miller, 1981.

17. Jacob, 1981, p. 130.

18. Fiorina, 1981.

19. A. Miller and Wattenberg, 1981. See also W. Miller, 1981; Markus, 1981; Petrocik, Verba, and Schultz, 1981; Burnham, 1981; and Abramson, Aldrich, and Rhode, 1982.

20. Ibid.

21. W. Miller, 1981, p. 39.

22. Campbell, 1960. See Hinckley, 1981, for an application of the various explanatory approaches to congressional elections.

23. Tufte, 1975; Pierson, 1975; Owens and Olson, 1980; Kuklinski and West, 1981; Kernell, 1977; Kritzer and Eubank, 1979; Bloom and Price, 1975; and Arcelus and Meltzer, 1975.

24. Erikson, 1971; Cover and Mayhew, 1981; Cover, 1977; Ferejohn, 1977; Mann, 1978; Nelson, 1978/1979; Parker, 1980; and Payne, 1980.

25. Remarks of Joe Gaylord, Political Director, National Republican Congressional Committee, and Dottie Lynch, CBS News, at panel on "Economic Issues and Elections: A Practitioners' Roundtable," Annual Conference of the Midwest Association for Public Opinion Research, November 19–20, Chicago, Illinois, 1982.

26. Petrocik and Steeper, 1982, Table 3.

27. Ibid.

28. Ibid., Table 2.

Chapter 7. Parties at the National Level

1. Janda, 1980b.

2. See Janda, 1980b, pp. 343–344.

3. For two accounts of the incident, see Shribman, 1981; and Evans and Novak, 1981.

4. Quoted in Crotty, 1980a.

5. Ibid., p. 45.

6. Crotty, 1977, pp. 247–256.

7. Crotty, 1978.

8. Longley, 1981, pp. 84–85. See also Longley, 1980a; and Longley, 1980b.

9. Cotter and Bibby, 1980, p. 2.

10. Ibid., p. 9.

11. Republican National Finance Committee, 1982, p. 12.

12. Janda, 1981, p. 6.

13. Ibid.

14. Republican National Finance Committee, 1982.

15. Janda, 1982, p. 6. See also Harmel and Janda, 1982, pp. 112–116; and Conway, 1981.

16. Janda, 1982, p. 4.

17. Ibid.

Chapter 8. Parties at the State Level

1. Key, 1949, 1956.

2. Jewell and Olson, 1982, pp. 58–60. See also Huckshorn, 1980 and 1976.

3. See also the earlier work by Weber, 1969.

4. Cotter, Gibson, Bibby, and Huckshorn, 1981.

5. Bibby, Huckshorn, Gibson, and Cotter, 1981; and Gibson, Cotter, Bibby, and Huckshorn, 1981.

6. The 1980 state party data are from Crotty, 1982.

7. Cotter, Gibson, Biddy, and Huckshorn, 1980.

8. Ibid.

9. Ibid.

10. Gibson, *et al.*, 1981.

11. Biersack and Haeuser, 1981.

12. Ibid., p. 18.

Chapter 9. Local Parties

1. See the summary review in Sorauf, 1980, pp. 67–107.

2. Quoted in Hawley, 1973, pp. 9–10.

3. Goodman, 1980, p. 83.

4. Quoted in Lee, 1960, p. 25.

5. For different introductions to the area, see Lee, 1960; Hawley, 1973; Adrian, 1952; and Adrian and Williams, 1959.

6. Greenstein, 1970, pp. 66–67.

7. Ibid.

8. Hawley, 1973, p. 150.

9. Ibid.

10. Crotty, 1981b; Eldersveld, 1981; Hopkins, 1981; Marvick, 1981; and Murray and Tedin, 1981.

11. See Eldersveld, 1964; Marvick, 1980; Katz and Eldersveld, 1961; Marvick, 1981; and Eldersveld, 1981.

12. Gosnell, 1937, pp. 47–48.

13. Quoted in Rakove, 1979, p. 97.

14. Ibid., p. 108.

Chapter 10. *Presidential Selection: Reform and Its Consequences*

1. These events are discussed in Crotty, 1978. See also David, 1980.

2. See Crotty, 1983.

3. Longley, 1980b.

4. Crotty, 1983a.

5. See, for example, Havelick, 1982; Report of the Commission on the Presidential Nominating Process, 1982; and Duke University Forum on Presidential Nominations, 1981.

6. See Democratic National Committee, 1982.

7. Materials in this section have appeared in Crotty, 1983b. On the operations of the contemporary nominating system, see also Aldrich, 1980; and Marshall, 1981.

8. Rubin, 1980.

9. Materials in this section have appeared in Crotty, 1982a, pp. 5–12.

10. Quoted in Crotty, 1981a, p. 1.

11. Duke University Forum on Presidential Nominations, 1981.

12. Ibid.

13. Schneider and Lewis, 1980, p. 142.

Chapter 11. *Media Politics*

1. See Robinson, 1980; Patterson, 1980; Graber, 1980. On campaign coverage, see Crouse, 1972.

2. Gans, 1979, pp. 94–95.

3. Graber, 1980, p. 179.

4. Ibid.

5. Crotty, 1984, pp. 89–97.

6. Lipinski, 1982.

7. Ibid.

8. Graber, 1980, p. 33.

9. Rubin, 1981, pp. 160–161.

10. Patterson and McClure, 1980, pp. 330–331. See also Patterson and McClure, 1976; and Patterson, 1980.

11. Ibid., p. 332.

12. Ibid., p. 333.

13. Rubin, 1967, p. 34.

14. Ibid.

15. Diamond, 1981, p. 174.

16. Ibid., p. 178.

17. Ibid.

18. Ibid., p. 173.

19. Ibid., pp. 173–4.

20. Ibid., p. 179.

21. Ibid.

Chapter 12.   Campaign Finance and the Rise of PACs

1. Bonafede, 1981, p. 50.

2. Ibid.

3. Orren, 1981, p. 53.

4. Bibby, Mann, and Ornstein, 1980, pp. 22–23.

5. The best account of these laws and the changes over time are in Alexander, 1980.

6. Gailey, 1982a, p. 12.

7. Epstein, 1980, p. 143.

8. Hucker, 1980.

9. Handler and Mulkorn, 1981.

10. Malbin, 1980, pp. 160–161.

11. Ibid., p. 162.

12. Gailey, 1982b.

13. Ibid.

14. Ibid.

15. Ibid.

16. Ibid.

17. Ibid.

18. Ibid.

19. Epstein, 1980, p. 144.

20. Viguerie, 1980, p. 5.

21. Ibid., p. 187.

22. Ibid., p. 183.

Chatper 13.   Conclusion: Revisionist Thoughts on Political Parties

1. American Political Science Association, 1950.

2. Crotty, 1977.

3. Crotty, 1980d.

BIBLIOGRAPHY

ABRAMSON, PAUL R., JOHN H. ALDRICH, and DAVID W. RHODE. *Change and Continuity in the 1980 Elections.* Washington, D.C.: Congressional Quarterly Press, 1982.

ABRAMSON, PAUL R., and JOHN H. ALDRICH. "The Decline of Electoral Participation in America." Paper delivered at the Annual Meeting of the American Political Science Association, New York City, 1981.

ADRIAN, CHARLES. "Some General Characteristics of Nonpartisan Elections." *American Political Science Review* 46 (September 1952: 766–776.

ADRIAN, CHARLES, and OLIVER WILLIAMS. "The Insulation of Local Politics under the Nonpartisan Ballot." *American Political Science Review* 53 (December 1959): 1052–1063.

ALDRICH, JOHN. *Before the Convention.* Chicago: University of Chicago Press, 1980.

ALEXANDER, HERBERT E. *Money in Politics.* Washington, D.C.: Public Affairs Press, 1972.

ALEXANDER, HERBERT E. *Political Finance,* 2d ed. Washington, D.C.: Congressional Quarterly Press, 1980.

ALEXANDER, HERBERT E. *Financing Politics,* 2d ed. Washington, D.C.: Congressional Quarterly Press, 1980.

AMERICAN POLITICAL SCIENCE ASSOCIATION. *Towards a More Responsible Two-Party System.* New York: Rinehart, 1950.

189

ANDERSEN, KRISTI. *The Creation of a Democratic Majority, 1928–1936.* Chicago: University of Chicago Press, 1979.

ARCELUS, F., and A. H. MELTZER. "The Effect of Aggregate Economic Variables on Congressional Elections." *American Political Science Review* (December 1975): 1232–1239. See also pp. 1255–1266.

ASHER, HERBERT B. *Presidential Elections and American Politics: Voters, Candidates and Campaigns since 1952,* rev. ed. Homewood, Ill: Dorsey Press, 1980.

AXELROD, ROBERT. "Where the Votes Come From: An Analysis of Electoral Coalitions, 1952–1968." *American Political Science Review* 66 (March 1972): 11–20.

BASS, JACK, and WALTER DEVRIES. *The Transformation of Southern Politics.* New York: Meridian Books, 1977.

BIBBY, JOHN F. "Comparative Study of State Political Parties." Paper delivered at the Conference on Political Parties in Modern Societies, Evanston, Illinois, 1978.

BIBBY, JOHN F., THOMAS E. MANN, and NORMAN J. ORNSTEIN. *Vital Statistics on Congress, 1980.* Washington, D.C.: American Enterprise Institute for Public Policy Research, 1980.

BIBBY, JOHN F., et al. "State Party Chairman Role Orientations and Institutional Party Strength." Paper delivered at the Annual Meeting of the Western Political Science Association, Denver, 1981.

BIERSACK, ROBERT W., and PATRICIA HAEUSER. "Political Party Organizations and Campaign Services to Candidates." Paper delivered at the Annual Meeting of the Midwest Political Science Association, Cincinnati, 1981.

BLOOM, H., and H. PRICE. "Voter Response to Short Run Economic Conditions: The Asymmetric Effect of Prosperity and Recession." *American Political Science Review* (December 1975): 1240–1254.

BONAFEDE, DOM. "A $130 Million Spending Tab Is Proof Presidential Politics Is Big Business." *National Journal* (January 10, 1981): 50–52.

BRODY, RICHARD A., and BENJAMIN I. PAGE. "Comment: The Assessment of Policy Voting." *American Political Science Review* 66 (June 1972): 450–458.

BRODY, RICHARD A., and BENJAMIN I. PAGE. "The Assessment of Policy Voting," in *Controversies in American Voting Behavior,* Richard G. Niemi and Herbert F. Weisberg, eds. San Francisco: W. H. Freeman, 1976.

BURNHAM, WALTER DEAN. *Critical Elections and the Mainsprings of American Politics.* New York: Norton, 1970.

BURNHAM, WALTER DEAN. "The Changing Shape of the American Political Universe," in *Controversies in American Voting Behavior*, Richard G. Niemi and Herbert F. Weisberg, eds. San Francisco: W. H. Freeman, 1976, pp. 451–483.

BURNHAM, WALTER DEAN. "The Appearance and Disappearance of the American Voter: An Historical Overview." Paper delivered at the Conference on the Future of the American Political System: What Can Be Done to Make It Work More Democratically and Effectively. Center for the Study of Democratic Politics, University of Pennsylvania, Philadelphia, 1979.

BURNHAM, WALTER DEAN. "The 1980 Earthquake: Realignment, Reaction, or What?" in *The Hidden Election*, Thomas Ferguson and Joel Rogers, eds. New York: Pantheon, 1981, pp. 98–140.

CADDELL, PATRICK H. "The Democratic Strategy and Its Electoral Consequences," in *Party Coalitions in the 1980s*, Seymour Martin Lipset, ed. San Francisco: Institute for Contemporary Studies, 1981, pp. 267–303.

CAMPBELL, BRUCE A. *The American Electorate: Attitudes and Actions*. New York: Holt, Rinehart and Winston, 1979.

CAMPBELL, BRUCE A., and RICHARD J. TRILLING, eds. *Realignment in American Politics*. Austin, Tex.: University of Texas Press, 1980.

CAMPBELL, ANGUS, PHILIP E. CONVERSE, WARREN E. MILLER, and DONALD E. STOKES. *The American Voter*. New York: John Wiley and Sons, 1960.

CAVANAGH, THOMAS E. "Changes in American Electoral Turnout, 1964–1976." *Political Science Quarterly* 96 (Spring 1981): 53–65.

CAVANAGH, THOMAS E. "Changes in American Electoral Turnout, 1964–1976." Paper delivered at the Annual Meeting of the Midwest Political Science Association, Chicago, 1979.

CAVANAGH, THOMAS E. "Research on American Voter Turnout: The State of the Evidence." Paper prepared for the Conference on Voter Participation, Washington, D.C., 1981.

COHEN, JEFFREY E., PATRICK R. COTTER, and PHILLIP B. COULTER. "Black Political Participation in Alabama: Matthews and Prothro Twenty Years Later." Paper delivered at the Southern Political Science Association Meetings, 1981.

COMMISSION ON THE PRESIDENTIAL NOMINATING PROCESS. *Report of the Commission on the Presidential Nominating Process*. Washington, D.C.: University Press of America, 1982.

CONVERSE, PHILLIP E. *The Dynamics of Party Support*. Beverly Hills, Cal.: Sage, 1976.

CONVERSE, PHILLIP E. "The Stability of Belief Elements over Time," in *Controversies in American Voting Behavior*, Richard G. Niemi and Herbert F. Weisberg, eds. San Francisco: W. H. Freeman, 1976.

CONVERSE, PHILLIP E. "The 'Responsible Electorate' of 1968," in *Controversies in American Voting Behavior*, Richard G. Niemi and Herbert F. Weisberg, eds. San Francisco: W. H. Freeman, 1976.

CONWAY, M. MARGARET. "Political Party Nationalization, Campaign Activities, and Local Party Development." Paper delivered at the Midwest Political Science Association Meeting, Cincinnati, 1981.

COTTER, CORNELIUS P., JAMES L. GIBSON, JOHN F. BIBBY, and ROBERT J. HUCKSHORN. "State Party Organizations and the Thesis of Party Decline." Paper delivered at the Annual Meeting of the American Political Science Association, Washington, D.C., 1980.

COTTER, CORNELIUS P., and JOHN F. BIBBY. "Institutional Development of Parties and the Thesis of Party Decline." *Political Science Quarterly*. 95 (Spring 1980): 1–27.

COTTER, CORNELIUS P., et al. "Party Organization, Electoral Success and Public Policy: An Analysis of Reciprocal Effects." Paper delivered at the Annual Meeting of the Southern Political Science Association, Memphis, 1981.

COVER, A. "One Good Term Deserves Another: The Advantage of Incumbency in Congressional Elections." *American Journal of Political Science* (August 1977): 523–542.

COVER, A., and MAYHEW, D. "Congressional Dynamics and the Decline of Competitive Congressional Elections," in *Congress Reconsidered*, 2 ed., L. Dodd and B. Oppenheimer, eds., Washington, D.C.: Congressional Quarterly, 1981, pp. 62–82.

CROTTY, WILLIAM. *Political Reform and the American Experiment*. New York: Thomas Y. Crowell, 1977.

CROTTY, WILLIAM. *Decision for the Democrats*. Baltimore: Johns Hopkins Press, 1978.

CROTTY, WILLIAM. "The National Committees as Grass-Roots Vehicles of Representation," in *The Party Symbol*, William Crotty, ed. San Francisco: W. H. Freeman, 1980, 35–49.

CROTTY, WILLIAM ed. *Paths to Political Reform*. Lexington, Mass.: Lexington Books, D. C. Heath, 1980b.

CROTTY, WILLIAM. "The Franchise: Registration Changes and Voter Representation," in *Paths to Political Reform*, William Crotty, ed. Lexington, Mass.: Lexington Books, D. C. Heath, 1980c, 67–113.

CROTTY, WILLIAM. "The Philosophies of Party Reform." in *Party Renewal in America*, Gerald M. Pomper, ed. New York: Praeger, 1980d, 31–50.

CROTTY, WILLIAM. "In Favor of the Status Quo." Paper prepared for the Conference on Presidential Selection of the American Bar Association's Committee on Election Law and Voter Participation, Racine, Wisconsin, July 1981a.

CROTTY, WILLIAM. "Local Party Organization in Chicago: The Machine Continues." Paper delivered at the Annual Meeting of the American Political Science Association, New York, 1981b.

CROTTY, WILLIAM. "'Improving' Presidential Selection." *Common Sense* 4 (2):5–12, 1982a.

CROTTY, WILLIAM. "Political Financing and State Party Organizational Effectiveness." Paper prepared for delivery at the Meeting of the International Political Science Association, Rio de Janeiro, 1982b.

CROTTY, WILLIAM. *Party Reform*. New York: Longman, 1983a.

CROTTY, WILLIAM. "The Presidential Nominating Campaigns," in *The Presidential Election of 1980 in State and Nation*, Paul David and David Everson, eds. Carbondale, Ill.: Southern Illinois University Press, 1983b, pp. 1–26.

CROTTY, WILLIAM. *American Parties in Decline*. Boston: Little, Brown, 1984.

CROUSE, TIMOTHY. *The Boys on the Bus*. New York: Random House, 1972.

DAVID, PAUL T. "Presidential-Nominee Selection: Primaries, Caucuses, and the National Convention," in *Paths to Political Reform*, William Crotty, ed. Lexington, Mass: Lexington Books, D. C. Heath, 1980, pp. 207–238.

DIAMOND, EDWIN. "The Ford and Carter Commercials They Didn't Dare Run," in *Watching American Politics*, Don Nimmo and William L. Rivers, eds. New York: Longman, 1981: 173–189.

DEMOCRATIC NATIONAL COMMITTEE. *Report of the Commission on Presidential Nomination*. Washington, D.C.: Democratic National Committee, 1982.

DENNIS, JACK. "Trends in Public Support for the American Party System." *British Journal of Political Science* 5 (April 1976): 187–230.

DENNIS, JACK. "Changing Public Support for the American Party System." in *Paths to Political Reform*, William Crotty, ed. Lexington, Mass.: Lexington Books, D. C. Heath, 1980, pp. 35–66.

DUKE UNIVERSITY FORUM ON PRESIDENTIAL NOMINATIONS. *A Statement of Purpose for Political Parties*. Durham, N.C.: The Duke University Forum, 1981.

ELDERSVELD, SAMUEL J. *Political Parties*. Chicago: Rand McNally, 1964.

ELDERSVELD, SAMUAL J. "The Party Activist in Detroit and Los Angeles: A Longitudinal View 1965–1980. Paper delivered at the Annual Meeting of the American Political Science Association, New York, 1981.

EPSTEIN, EDWIN M. "Business and Labor under the Federal Election Campaign Act of 1971." in *Parties, Interest Groups, and Campaign Finance Laws*, Michael J. Malbin, ed. Washington, D.C.: American Enterprise Institute for Public Policy Research, 1980, pp. 107–151.

ERIKSON, R. "The Advantage of Incumbency in Congressional Elections." *Polity* 3 (Spring 1971): 395–405.

EVANS, ROWLAND, and ROBERT NOVAK. "Ax GOP Chief Richards, Install Laxalt, Reagan Told." *Chicago Sun-Times* (December 10, 1981): 34.

FEE, JOAN L. "Religion, Ethnicity, and Class in American Electoral Behavior," in *The Party Symbol*, William Crotty, ed. San Francisco: W. H. Freeman, 1980, pp. 257–273.

FEREJOHN, J. "On the Decline of Competition in Congressional Elections." *American Political Science Review* 71 (March 1977): 166–176.

FIORINA, MORRIS P. *Retrospective Voting in American National Elections.* New Haven: Yale University Press, 1981.

FLANIGAN, WILLIAM H., and NANCY H. ZINGALE. *Political Behavior of the American Electorate.* Boston: Allyn and Bacon, 1979.

FLEISHMAN, JOEL, ed. *The Future of American Political Parties.* New York: Columbia University, The American Assembly, 1982.

FRANKOVIC, KATHLEEN A. "Public Opinion Trends," in *The Election of 1980*, G. Pomper, ed. Chatham, N.J.: Chatham House, 1981, pp. 97–118.

FREED, BRUCE F. "Political Money and Campaign Finance Reform, 1971–1978," in *Parties and Elections in an Anti-Party Age*, Jeff Fishel, ed. Bloomington: Indiana University Press, 1978, pp. 241–255.

GAILEY, PHIL. "Election Unit's Tasks: Udall and Lance Cases," *The New York Times* (February 17, 1982a): 12.

GALLEY, PHIL. "A Political Action Unit of the Left," *The New York Times* (February 10, 1982b): 11.

GANS, HERBERT J. *Deciding What's News.* New York: Patheon, 1979.

GIBSON, JAMES L., CORNELIUS P. COTTER, JOHN F. BIBBY, and ROBERT J. HUCKSHORN. "Assessing Institutional Party Strength." Paper delivered at the Annual Meeting of the Midwest Political Science Association, Cincinnati, 1981.

GOODMAN, WILLIAM. *The Party System in America.* Englewood Cliffs, N.J.: Prentice-Hall, 1980.

GOSNELL, HAROLD F. *Machine Politics: Chicago Model.* Chicago: University of Chicago Press, 1937.

GRABER, DORIS A. *Mass Media and American Politics.* Washington, D.C.: Congressional Quarterly Press, 1980.

GREENSTEIN, FRED I. *The American Party System and the American People,* 2d ed. Englewood Cliffs, N.J.: Prentice-Hall, 1970.

HANDLER, EDWARD, and JOHN MULKERN. "A Comparative Analysis of Corporate PAC Campaign Contribution Strategies in the Congressional Elections of 1978 and 1980." Paper delivered at the Annual Meeting of the American Political Science Association, New York, 1981.

HARMEL, ROBERT, and KENNETH JANDA. *Parties and Their Environments: The Limits to Reform.* New York: Longman, 1982.

HAVARD, WILLIAM C., ed. *The Changing Politics of the South.* Baton Rouge, Louisiana State University Press, 1972.

HAVELICK, FRANKLIN J., ed. *Presidential Selection.* New York: American Bar Association Special Committee on Election Law and Voter Participation, 1982.

HAWLEY, WILLIS D. *Nonpartisan Elections.* New York: Wiley, 1973.

HERSHEY, MARJORIE RANDON, and DARNEL M. WEST. "Single-Issue Groups and Political Campaigns: Six Senatorial Races and the Pro-Life Challenge in 1980." Paper delivered at the Annual Meeting of the Midwest Political Science Association, Cincinnati, 1981.

HINCKLEY, BARBARA. *Congressional Elections.* Washington, D.C.: Congressional Quarterly Press, 1981.

HOPKINS, ANNE H. "Local Party Organization in Nashville: Border State Democrats." Paper delivered at the Annual Meeting of the American Political Science Association, New York, 1981.

HUCKER, CHARLES W. "Explosive Growth: Corporate Political Action Committees are Less Oriented to Republicans Than Expected," in *The Party Symbol,* William Crotty, ed. San Francisco: W. H. Freeman, 1980, pp. 306–315.

HUCKSHORN, ROBERT J. *Party Leadership in the States.* Amherst, Mass.: University of Massachusetts Press, 1976.

HUCKSHORN, ROBERT J. "The Role of Orientations of State Party Chairmen," in *The Party Symbol,* William Crotty, ed. San Francisco: W. H. Freeman, 1980.

JACKSON, JOHN E. "Issues, Party Choices, and Presidential Votes." *American Journal of Political Sciences* 19(2) (May 1975): 161–185.

JACOB, CHARLES E. "The Congressional Elections," in *The Election of 1980,* Gerald M. Pomper, ed. Chatham, N.J.: Chatham House, 1981, pp. 119–141.

JACOBSON, GARY C., and SAMUEL KERNELL. *Strategy and Choice in Congressional Elections.* New Haven: Yale University Press, 1981.

JANDA, KENNETH. *Political Parties: A Cross-National Survey.* New York: Free Press, 1980a.

JANDA, KENNETH. "A Comparative Analysis of Party Organizations: The United States, Europe, and the World," in *The Party Symbol*, William Crotty, ed. San Francisco: W. H. Freeman, 1980b, pp. 339–358.

JANDA, KENNETH. "Let's Have a Party: The Republican Presence in the 1981 Election." Paper presented at the Annual Meeting of the Illinois Political Science Association, Chicago, 1981.

JENSEN, RICHARD. "Party Coalitions and the Search for Modern Values: 1820–1970," in *Party Coalitions in the 1980s*, Seymour Martin Lipset, ed. San Francisco: Institute for Contemporary Studies, 1981.

JEWELL, MALCOLM, E., and DAVID M. OLSON. *American State Political Parties and Elections*, rev. ed. Homewood, Ill.: The Dorsey Press, 1982.

KAGAY, MICHAEL R., and GREG A. CALDEIRA. "A 'Reformed' Electorate? Well, at Least a Changed Electorate," in *Paths to Political Reform*, William Crotty, ed. Lexington, Mass.: D. C. Heath, 1980, pp. 3–33.

KATZ, DANIEL, and SAMUEL J. ELDERSVELD. "The Impact of Local Party Activity upon the Electorate." *Public Opinion Quarterly* 25 (1961): 1–24.

KEEFE, WILLIAM J. *Parties, Politics, and Public Policy in America*, 3rd ed. New York: Holt, Rinehart and Winston, 1980.

KERNELL, S. "Presidential Popularity and Negative Voting." *American Political Science Review* 71 (March 1977): 44–66.

KEY, V. O., Jr. *Southern Politics.* New York: Knopf, 1949.

KEY, V. O., Jr. *American State Politics: An Introduction.* New York: Knopf, 1956.

KEY, V. O. Jr. *The Responsible Electorate: Rationality in Presidential Voting, 1936–1960.* Cambridge, Mass.: Harvard University Press, 1966.

KINDER, DONALD R., and ROBERT P. ABELSON. "Appraising Presidential Candidates: Personality and Affect in the 1980 Campaign." Paper delivered at the Annual Meeting of the American Political Science Association, New York, 1981.

KLEPPNER, PAUL. "Coalitional and Party Transformations in the 1890s," in *Party Coalitions in the 1980s*, Seymour Martin Lipset, ed. San Francisco: Institute for Contemporary Studies, 1981.

KRITZER, H., and R. EUBANK. "Presidential Coattails Revisited: Partisanship and Incumbency Effects." *American Journal of Political Science* 23 (August 1979): 616–625.

KUKLINSKI, J., and D. WEST. "Economic Expectations and Mass Voting in United States House and Senate Elections." *American Political Science Review* (June 1981).

LADD, EVERETT CARLL, Jr. "Liberalism Upside Down: The Inversion of the New Deal Order." *Political Science Quarterly* 91 (Winter 1976–1977): 577–600.

LADD, EVERETT CARLL, Jr., and CHARLES D. HADLEY. *Transformations of the American Party System*. New York: Norton, 1975.

LEE, EUGENE C. *The Politics of Nonpartisanship*. Berkeley, Cal.: University of California Press, 1960.

LIPINSKI, ANN MARIE. "Show Biz and the News: Agents Meet the Press." *Chicago Tribune* (February 3, 1982) section 2: 1.

LONGLEY, CHARLES. "National Party Renewal," in *Party Renewal in America*, Gerald M. Pomper, ed. New York: Praeger, 1980, pp. 69–86.

LONGLEY, CHARLES. "Party Nationalization in America," In *Paths to Political Reform*, William Crotty, ed. Lexington, Mass.: Lexington Books, D. C. Heath, 1980a, pp. 167–205.

LONGLEY, CHARLES. "Party Reform and Party Nationalization: The Case of the Democrats," in *The Party Symbol*, William Crotty, ed. San Francisco: W. H. Freeman, 1980b.

LUTTBEG, NORMAN R. "Declining Turnout 1960–1980: Does it Depend on the State?" Paper delivered at the Annual Meeting of the Southern Political Science Association, Memphis, 1981.

MACDOUGAL, MALCOLM. *We Almost Made It*. New York: Crown, 1977.

MADDOX, WILLIAM. "The Changing American Nonvoter," in *Watching American Politics*, Dan Nimmo and William L. Rivers, eds. New York: Longman, 1981.

MALBIN, MICHAEL J. "Of Mountains and Molehills: PACs, Campaigns, and Public Policy," in *Parties, Interest Groups, and Campaign Finance Laws*, Michael J. Malbin, ed. Washington, D.C.: American Enterprise Institute for Public Policy Research, 1980, pp. 152–184.

MANN, T. *Unsafe At Any Margin*. Washington, D.C.: American Enterprise Institute, 1978.

MARGOLIS, MICHAEL. "From Confusion to Confusion: Issues and the American Voter." *American Political Science Review* 71 (March 1977): 31–43.

MARKUS, GREGORY B. "Political Attitudes During an Election Year: A Report on the 1980 NES Panel Study." Paper delivered at the Annual Meeting of the American Political Science Association, New York, 1981.

MARSHALL, THOMAS R. *Presidential Nominations in a Reform Age.* New York: Praeger, 1981.

MARVICK, DWAINE. "Party Organizational Personnel and Electoral Democracy in Los Angeles, 1963–1972," in *The Party Symbol*, William Crotty, ed. San Francisco: W. H. Freeman, 1980, pp. 63–86.

MARVICK, DWAINE. "Local Partisan Organizational Effects in Los Angeles: Contrasts in Campaign Activity in 1980." Paper delivered at the Annual Meeting of the American Political Science Association, New York, 1981.

MATASAR, ANN B. "Corporate Responsibility Gone Awry? The Corporate Political Action Committee." Paper delivered at the Annual Meeting of the American Political Science Association, New York, 1981.

MAZMANIAN, DANIEL A. *Third Parties in Presidential Elections.* Washington, D.C.: The Brookings Institution, 1974.

MCDONALD, STEPHEN L. "Economic Issues in the Campaign," in *A Tide of Discontent*, Ellis Sandoz and Cecil V. Crabb, eds. Washington, D.C.: Congressional Quarterly Press, 1981.

MCGINNISS, JOE. *The Selling of the President, 1968.* New York: Trident Press, 1969.

MERRION, PAUL. "Illinois PACs Face Tough Choices in '82 Races." *Crain's Chicago Business* (January 25, 1982): 13–16.

MILLER, Arthur H. "Political Issues and Trust in Government: 1964–1970." *American Political Science Review* 68 (September 1974): 951–972.

MILLER, ARTHUR H., and WARREN E. MILLER. "Partisanship and Performance: 'Rational' Choice in the 1976 Presidential Election." Paper delivered at the Annual Meeting of the American Political Science Association, Washington, D.C., 1977.

MILLER, ARTHUR H. "Partisanship Reinstated? A Comparison of the 1972 and 1976 U.S. Presidential Elections." *British Journal of Political Science* 1978.

MILLER, ARTHUR H., WARREN E. MILLER, ALDEN S. RAINE, and THAD A. BROWN. "A Majority Party in Disarray: Policy Polarization in the 1972 Election," In *Controversies in American Voting Behavior*, Richard G. Niemi and Herbert F. Weisberg, San Francisco: W. H. Freeman, 1976: pp. 176–195.

MILLER, ARTHUR H., and MARTIN P. WATTENBERG. "Policy and Performance Voting in the 1980 Election." Paper delivered at the Annual Meeting of the American Political Science Association, New York, 1981.

MILLER, WARREN E. "Policy Directions and Presidential Leadership: Alternative Interpretations of the 1980 Presidential Election." Paper delivered at the Annual Meeting of the American Political Science Association, New York, 1981.

MILLER, WARREN E., ARTHUR H. MILLER, and EDWARD J. SCHNEIDER. *American National Election Studies Data Sourcebook. 1952–1978*. Cambridge, Mass.: Harvard University Press, 1980.

MURRAY, RICHARD, and KENT TEDIN. "Local Party Organization in Houston." Paper delivered at the Annual Meeting of the American Political Science Association, New York, 1981.

NELSON, C. "The Effect of Incumbency on Voting in Congressional Elections." *Political Science Quarterly* (Winter 1978–1979): 665–678.

NIE, NORMAN H., SIDNEY VERBA, and JOHN R. PETROCIK. *The Changing American Voter*. Cambridge, Mass.: Harvard University Press, 1976.

NIMMO, DAN. *Political Communication and Public Opinion in America*. Santa Monica, Cal.: Goodyear, 1978.

ORNSTEIN, NORMAN J., THOMAS E. MANN, MICHAEL J. MALBIN, and JOHN F. BIBBY. *Vital Statistics on Congress*. Washington, D.C.: American Enterprise Institute, 1982.

ORREN, GARY R. "Presidential Campaign Finance: Its Impact and Future," in *Common Sense*. Washington, D.C.: Republican National Committee, 1981, pp. 50–66.

OWENS, J., and E. OLSON. "Economic Fluctuations and Congressional Elections." *American Journal of Political Science* 24 (August 1980): 469–493.

PAGE, BENJAMIN I. *Choices and Echoes in Presidential Elections*. Chicago: University of Chicago Press, 1978.

PARKER, G. "The Advantage of Incumbency in House Elections." *American Politics Quarterly* 8 (October 1980): 449–464.

PATTERSON, THOMAS E. *The Mass Media Election*. New York: Praeger, 1980.

PATTERSON, THOMAS E., and ROBERT D. MCCLURE. *The Unseeing Eye*. New York: Putnam, 1976.

PATTERSON, THOMAS E., and ROBERT D. MCCLURE. "Television and Voter's Issue Awareness," in *The Party Symbol*, William Crotty, ed. San Francisco: W. H. Freeman, 1980, pp. 324–334.

PAYNE, J. "The Personal Electoral Advantage of House Incumbents, 1936–1976." *American Politics Quarterly* 8 (October 1980): 465–482.

PENNIMAN, HOWARD R. "Presidential Third Parties and the Modern American Two-Party System," in *The Party Symbol*, William Croty, ed. San Francisco: W. H. Freeman, 1980, pp. 101–117.

PETROCIK, JOHN R. *Party Coalitions: Realignment and the Decline of the New Deal Party System*. Chicago: University of Chicago Press, 1981.

PETROCIK, JOHN R., and FRED T. STEEPER. "Economic Issues and the Local Candidate in the 1982 Congressional Election." Paper delivered at the Annual Meeting of the Midwest Association for Public Opinion Research, Chicago, 1981.

PETROCIK, JOHN R., SIDNEY VERBA, and CHRISTINE SCHULTZ. "Choosing the Choice and Not the Echo: A Funny Thing Happened to *The Changing American Voter* on the way to the 1980 Election." Paper delivered at the Annual Meeting of the American Political Science Association, New York, 1961.

PIERESON, J. "Presidential Popularity and Midterm Voting at Different Election Levels." *American Journal of Political Science* (November 1975): 683–694.

POMPER, GERALD M. *Voter's Choice.* New York: Dodd, Mead, 1975.

POMPER, GERALD M. "The Presidential Election," in *The Election of 1976,* Gerald M. Pomper, ed. New York: McKay, 1977.

POMPER, GERALD M. "The Nominating Contests," in *The Election of 1980,* Gerald M. Pomper, ed. Chatham, N.J.: Chatham House, 1981, pp. 1–37.

POMPER, GERALD M. "The Presidential Election," in *The Election of 1980,* Gerald M. Pomper, ed. Chatham, N.J.: Chatham House, 1981, pp. 65–96.

RAKOVE, MILTON L. *We Don't Want Nobody Nobody Sent.* Bloomington: Indiana University Press, 1979.

REPUBLICAN NATIONAL COMMITTEE. *1981 Republican Almanac.* Washington, D.C.: Communications Division, Republican National Committee, 1981.

REPUBLICAN NATIONAL FINANCE COMMITTEE. *1981 Chairman's Report.* Washington, D.C.: Republican National Committee, 1982.

ROBINSON, MICHAEL J. "Media Coverage in the Primary Campaign of 1976: Implications for Voters, Candidates, and Parties," in *The Party Symbol,* William Crotty, ed. San Francisco: W. H. Freeman, 1980, pp. 178–191.

ROBINSON, MICHAEL J. "The Media in 1980: Was the Message the Message?" in *The American Elections of 1980,* Austin Ranney, ed. Washington, D.C.: American Enterprise Institute, 1981, pp. 177–211.

ROSENSTONE, STEVEN J., ROY L. BEHR, and EDWARD H. LAZARUS. "Third Party Voting in America." Paper delivered at the Annual Meeting of the American Political Science Association, New York, 1981.

RUBIN, BERNARD. *Political Television.* Belmont, Cal.: Wadsworth, 1967.

RUBIN, RICHARD L. "Presidential Primaries: Continuities, Dimensions of Change, and Political Implications," in *The Party Symbol*, William Crotty, ed. W. H. Freeman, 1980, pp. 126–147.

RUBIN, RICHARD L. *Press, Party, and Presidency*. New York: Norton, 1981.

RUSK, JERROLD G. "The Effect of the Australian Ballot Reform on Split Ticket Voting: 1876–1908," in *Controversies in American Voting Behavior*, Richard G. Niemi and Herbert F. Weisberg, eds. San Francisco: W. H. Freeman, 1976.

SANDOZ, ELLIS, and CECIL V. CRABB, Jr., eds. *A Tide of Discontent*. Washington, D.C.: Congressional Quarterly Press, 1981.

SCAMMON, RICHARD M., and BEN J. WATTENBERG. "A New Tide Observed: The Social Issue," in *Controversies in American Voting Behavior*, Richard G. Niemi and Herbert F. Weisberg, eds. San Francisco: W. H. Freeman, 1976.

SCHATTSCHNEIDER, E. E. *Party Government*. New York: Rinehart, 1942.

SCHATTSCHNEIDER, E. E. *The Semi-Soverign People*. New York: Holt, Rinehart, 1960.

SCHNEIDER, WILLIAM. "The November 4 Vote for President: What Did It Mean?," in *The American Elections of 1980*, Austin Ranney, ed. Washington, D.C.: American Enterprise Institute, 1981, pp. 212–262.

SCHNEIDER, WILLIAM. "Democrats and Republicans, Liberals and Conservatives," in *Party Coalitions in the 1980s*, Seymore Martin Lipset, ed. San Francisco: Institute for Contemporary Studies, 1981.

SELLERS, CHARLES. "The Equilibrium Cycle in Two-Party Politics," in *Political Parties and Political Behavior*, William Crotty, Donald M. Freeman, and Douglas S. Gatlin, eds. Boston: Allyn and Bacon, 1966, pp. 79–102.

SHRIBMAN, DAVID. "Bush Aide Chosen for G.O.P. Position." *New York Times* (December 11, 1981): 12.

SORAUF, FRANK J. *Party Politics in America*. 4th ed. Boston: Little, Brown, 1980.

STANLEY, HAROLD W. "Explaining Electoral Mobilization: White Southerners and Racial Backlash, 1952–1980." Paper delivered at the Annual Meeting of the Southern Political Science Association, Memphis, 1981a.

STANLEY, HAROLD W. "The Political Impact of Electoral Mobilization: The South and Universal Suffrage, 1952–1980." Paper delivered at the Annual Meeting of the American Political Science Association, New York, 1981b.

201

SUNDQUIST, JAMES L. *Dynamics of the Party System.* Washington, D.C.: Brooklings Institution, 1973.

TUFTE, E. "Determinants of the Outcome of Midterm Congressional Elections." *American Political Science Review* 69 (September 1975): 812–826.

VIGUERIE, RICHARD A. *The New Right: We're Ready to Lead.* Falls Church, Va.: The Viguerie Company, 1980.

WEBER, RONALD E. "Competitive and Organizational Dimensions of American State Party Systems." Paper delivered at the Meeting of the Northeastern Political Science Association, Hartford, CT, 1969.

WEINBERG, LEE, et al., "Local Party Organization: From Disaggregation to Disintegration." Paper delivered at the Annual Meeting of the American Political Science Association, Washington, D.C., 1980.

WIRTHLIN, RICHARD B. "The Republican Strategy and Its Electoral Consequences." In *Party Coalitions in the 1980s*, Seymour Martin Lipset, ed. San Francisco: Institute for Contemporary Studies, 1981: 235–266.

WOLFINGER, RAYMOND E., and STEVEN J. ROSENSTONE. *Who Votes?* New Haven, CT: Yale University Press, 1980.

Name Index

203

Subject Index